W9-ABI-184

NATIVE AMERICAN WOMEN WRITERS

NATIVE AMERICAN WOMEN WRITERS

Edited and with an Introduction by

Harold Bloom

CHELSEA HOUSE PUBLISHERS

Philadelphia

ON THE COVER: *Migration of the Parrot* by Linda Lomahaftawa, contemporary Native American artist. Acrylic on canvas. 1994.

CHELSEA HOUSE PUBLISHERS

EDITOR-IN-CHIEF   Stephen Reginald
MANAGING EDITOR   James D. Gallagher
PRODUCTION MANAGER   Pamela Loos
PICTURE EDITOR   Judy Hasday
ART DIRECTOR   Sara Davis
SENIOR PRODUCTION EDITOR   Lisa Chippendale

WOMEN WRITERS OF ENGLISH AND THEIR WORKS:
  Native American Women Writers

SERIES EDITOR   Jane Shumate
CONTRIBUTING EDITOR   Deborah Williams
SENIOR EDITOR   Therese De Angelis
COVER DESIGNERS   Sara Davis and Keith Trego
EDITORIAL ASSISTANT   Anne Hill

Introduction © 1998 by Harold Bloom

First Printing
1 3 5 7 9 8 6 4 2

Library of Congress Cataloging-in-Publication Data

Native American fiction writers / edited and with an introduction by
  Harold Bloom.
      126 p.   cm. — (Women writers of English and their works)
      Includes bibliographical references.
      ISBN 0-7910-4479-3 (hc). — ISBN 0-7910-4495-5 (pbk.)
      1. American literature—Indian authors—History and criticism.
   2. American literature—Women authors—History and criticism.
   3. Indian women—United States—Intellectual life. 4. Women and
   literature—United States—History. 5. Indians in literature.
   I. Bloom, Harold. II. Series.
   PS153. I52N38   1998
   810.9'9287'08997—dc21   97-40088
                                                        CIP

CONTENTS

THE ANALYSIS OF WOMEN WRITERS

HAROLD BLOOM

I APPROACH THIS SERIES with a certain wariness, since so much of classical feminist literary criticism has founded itself upon arguments with that phase of my own work that began with *The Anxiety of Influence* (first published in January 1973). Someone who has been raised to that bad eminence—*The Patriarchal Critic*—is well advised that he trespasses upon sacred ground when he ventures to inquire whether indeed there are indisputable differences, imaginative and cognitive, between the literary works of women and those of men. If these differences are so substantial as pragmatically to make an authentic difference, does that in turn make necessary different aesthetic standards for judging the achievements of men and of women writers? Is Emily Dickinson to be read as though she has more in common with Elizabeth Barrett Browning than with Ralph Waldo Emerson?

Is Elizabeth Bishop a great poet because she triumphantly meets the same aesthetic criteria satisfied by Wallace Stevens, or should we evaluate her by criteria she shares with Marianne Moore, but not with Stevens? Are there crucial gender-based differences in the representations of Esther Summerson by Charles Dickens in *Bleak House*, and of Dorothea Brooke by George Eliot in *Middlemarch*? Does Samuel Richardson's Clarissa Harlowe convince us that her author was a male when we contrast her with Jane Austen's Elizabeth Bennet? Do women poets have a less agonistic relationship to female precursors than male poets have to their forerunners? Two eminent pioneers of feminist criticism, Sandra Gilbert and Susan Gubar, have suggested that women writers suffer more from an anxiety of authorship than they do from influence anxieties, while another important feminist critic, Elaine Showalter, has suggested that women writers, early and late, work together in a kind of quiltmaking, each doing her share while avoiding any contamination of creative envy in regard to other writers, provided that they be women. Can it be true that, in the aesthetic sphere, women do not beware women and do not suffer from the competitiveness and jealousy that alas do exist in the professional and sexual domains? Is there something in the area of literature, when practiced by women, that changes and purifies mere human nature?

I cannot answer any of these questions, yet I do think it is vital and clarifying to raise them. There is a current fashion, in many of our institutions of higher education, to insist that English Romantic poetry cannot be studied in the old way, with an exclusive emphasis upon the works of William Blake, William Wordsworth, Samuel Taylor Coleridge, Lord Byron, Percy Bysshe Shelley, John Keats, and John Clare. Instead, the Romantic poets are taken to include Felicia Hemans, Laetitia Landon, Charlotte Smith, and Mary Tighe, among others. It would be heartening if we could believe that these are unjustly neglected poets, but their current revival will be brief. Similarly, anthologies of 17th-century English literature now tend to include the Duchess of Newcastle as well as Aphra Behn, Lady Mary Chudleigh, Anne Killigrew, Anne Finch, Countess of Winchilsea, and others. Some of these—Anne Finch in particular—wrote well, but a situation in which they are more read and studied than John Milton is not one that is likely to endure forever. The consequences of making gender a criterion for aesthetic choice must finally destroy all serious study of imaginative literature as such.

In their *Norton Anthology of Literature by Women*, Sandra Gilbert and Susan Gubar conclude their introduction to Elizabeth Barrett Browning by saying that "she constantly tested herself against the highest standards of male-defined poetic genres," a true if ambiguous observation. They then print her famous "The Cry of the Children," an admirably passionate ode that protests the cruel employment of little children in British Victorian mines and factories. Unfortunately, this well-meant prophetic affirmation ends with this, doubtless its finest stanza:

XIII
They look up with their pale and sunken faces,
    And their look is dread to see,
For they mind you of their angels in high places,
    With eyes turned on Deity.
"How long," they say, "how long, O cruel nation,
    Will you stand, to move the world, on a child's heart,—
Stifle down with a mailèd heel its palpitation,
    And tread onward to your throne amid the mart?
Our blood splashes upward, O goldheaper,
    And your purple shows your path!
But the child's sob in the silence curses deeper
    Than the strong man in his wrath."

If you read this aloud, then you may find yourself uncomfortable, on a strictly aesthetic basis, which would not vary if you were told that this had been composed by a male Victorian poet. In their selections from Elizabeth Bishop, Gilbert and Gubar courageously reprint Bishop's superb statement explaining her refusal to permit her poems to be included in anthologies of women's writing:

Undoubtedly gender does play an important part in the making of any art, but art is art and to separate writings, paintings, musical compositions, etc., into sexes is to emphasize values in them that are *not* art.

XII

That credo of Elizabeth Bishop's is to me the Alpha and Omega of critical wisdom in regard to all feminist literary criticism. Gender studies are precisely that: they study gender, and not aesthetic value. If your priorities are historical, social, political, and ideological, then gender studies clearly are more than justified. Perhaps they are a way to justice, or at least to more justice than women have received throughout thousands of years of male domination and aggression. Yet that is a very different matter from the now vexed issue of aesthetic value. Biographical criticism, like the different modes of historicist and psychological criticism, always has relied upon a kind of implicit gender studies and doubtless will benefit, as other modes will, by a making explicit of such considerations, particularly in regard to women writers.

Each volume in this series contains copious refutations of, and replies to, the traditionally aesthetic stance that I have advocated here. These introductory remarks aspire only to a questioning, and not a challenging, of feminist literary criticism. There are no longer any Patriarchal Critics; they are all dinosaurs, fabulous beasts fit for revival only in horror films. Sometimes I sadly think of myself as Bloom Brontosaurus, amiably left behind by the fire and the flood. But more often I go on reading the great women writers, searching for the aesthetic difference that yet may prove to be there, but which has not yet been found.

INTRODUCTION

LESLIE MARMON SILKO, partly Laguna Pueblo in her ancestry, is, with Louise Erdrich and Mourning Dove, one of the most widely read of Native American women writers. It is twenty years since her first novel, *Ceremony*, appeared, and still that seems to me her most poignant narrative fiction. Rather than examine it here, I prefer to meditate upon Silko's letters and poems in *The Delicacy and Strength of Lace: Letters between Leslie Marmon Silko and James Wright*, as edited by Anne Wright in 1986. Wright, a major American poet, died in 1980, just fifty-two: two of his volumes, *The Branch Will Not Break* and *Shall We Gather at the River?* seem to me part of the authentic American canon of this century. Silko, who has immense potential as a writer, necessarily manifests the moral necessity of protesting, in her work, the long persecution of the Native American peoples. Though this political burden is less dominant in *Ceremony* than in *Almanac of the Dead* (1991), where it somewhat weighs down Silko's narrative art, I find very refreshing *The Delicacy and Strength of Lace*, where the informal intimacy of the correspondence frees Silko from the politics of protest. Like James Wright, Silko is a superb letter-writer, maintaining always a fine balance between personal revelation and keen attention to the other's interests and horizons.

In an undated letter from Tucson, Silko sends Wright a "Note on the Deer Dance":

> In the fall the Laguna hunters go to the hills and mountains around Laguna Pueblo to bring back the deer. The people think of the deer as coming to give themselves to the hunters so that the people will have meat through the winter. Late in the winter the Deer Dance is performed to honor and pay thanks to the deer spirits who've come home with the hunters that year. Only when this has been properly done will the spirits be able to return to the mountain and be reborn into more deer who will, remembering the reverence and appreciation of the people, once more come home with the hunters.

The lovely phrase, "come home with the hunters," is repeated by Silko in the gracious lyric that follows:

> You have come home with me before
> a long way down the mountain.
> The people welcome you.
> I took
> the best red blanket for you
> the turquoise the silver rings

were very old
something familiar for you
blue corn and meal saved special.

While others are sleeping
I tie feathers on antlers
whisper close to you
      we have missed you
      I have longed for you.

Losses are certain
in the pattern of this dance.
Over the terrain a hunter travels
blind curves in the trail
seize the breath
until it leaps away
loose again
to run the hills.
      Go quickly.

    This poem of the Deer Dance has a remarkable tact: its resonance is at once so controlled and so suggestive that we could be reading a love lyric as well as a ritual celebration. So grave a ceremonial art represents Silko at her best and makes me half regret the most important social function of her writing, which is to increase awareness of a pattern of wrongs that has been neverending. Wright, in his first letter to Silko, calls *Ceremony* "one of the four or five best books I have ever read about America." That is generous overpraise, though *Ceremony* will continue to sustain many rereadings.

    In Silko's last letter to Wright (March 24, 1980), which arrived after his death, there is a marvelous visitation by an owl:

> After sundown the other night I was sitting on the road with Denny, and a great owl with eight-foot wings landed on a tall saguaro close to us. Jim, this owl was so big that, after he folded his wings, his size matched the diameter of the saguaro and he became part of the cactus top. It was only with the most careful concentration that I could see the owl swivel his head and thus believe that there was an owl sitting there. I thought about you then, Jim, as I always will when I am visited by the owls. He is probably the owl who carries off the cats the coyotes don't bother to catch, and after that night I was ready to believe this owl carries off whatever he damn well pleases.

    The emblem of wisdom "became part of the cactus top," blending into the scene yet remaining a real presence from without. Silko beautifully renders this into a tribute to her dying friend, always with her, but soon to be forever remote. Her sensibility is so acute that one finds oneself hoping yet again that she will abandon herself to an art of perception and sensation, even if it means neglecting, for a time, the sorrows of history and the inequities of America.

PAULA GUNN ALLEN

B. 1939

PAULA GUNN ALLEN was born in 1939 to a Laguna Pueblo mother and a Lebanese father. Allen herself is a member of the Laguna Pueblo, which can also claim Leslie Marmon Silko among its members; Silko is in fact Allen's cousin. Allen spent much of her childhood absorbing Pueblo stories and cultural beliefs. She later earned a Ph.D. in American studies from the University of New Mexico, in 1975.

Allen first came to national attention through her poetry, which she began writing in the 1960s, under the auspices of the poet Robert Creeley. Like the work of many other Native American writers, Allen's poetry moves between worlds, drawing on Catholicism, Laguna spirituality, her advanced education, and the stories she was told as a child. She counts among her literary influences the Romantic poets, particularly Shelley and Keats; Gertrude Stein; the Beat poets; and, more contemporaneously, the poets Audre Lorde, Adrienne Rich, and Denise Levertov. She has also said that N. Scott Momaday's book *House Made of Dawn* brought her back to herself, convincing her that her experiences as a Native woman could become the subject for her writing.

In *The Woman Who Owned the Shadows* (1983), Allen's first novel, she creates a racially mixed heroine, Ephanie, who must come to terms with her lesbianism through a vision quest (a form of self-discovery traditional to various Native groups). In Allen's words, Ephanie must move from thinking of her reference group as male to thinking of it as female. Ephanie must refeminize herself in what Allen says is the tribal way, rather than the Western way. In the Western way, according to Allen, a woman learns to expect a man to shape her life, rather than shaping it herself.

In addition to her poetry and fiction, Allen is well known for her scholarship, particularly in bringing Indian literature and writers to the attention of wider audiences. *Studies in American Indian Literature: Critical Essays and Course Designs* (1983) has been particularly instrumental in helping bring American Indian literature to the classroom. Her anthology *Spider Woman's Granddaughters* (1989), which won the American Book Award in 1990, is one of the first collections of short fiction by Native women writers. Although Allen has been crucial in bringing Native literature to a wider audience, she resists what she considers to be inappropriate intrusions into Native cultures.

Allen's lifelong commitment to the antiwar and antinuclear move-
ments and to American feminism are at the center of her work; she
continues to write, speak, and teach about the ritual traditions of
Native American women. She has taught at the University of
California, Berkeley, and currently teaches at UCLA. Her work has
brought her critical and popular acclaim, including grants and fellow-
ships from the National Endowment for the Arts (1978) and the
Native American Prize for Literature (1990).

CRITICAL EXTRACTS

KENNETH LINCOLN

Laguna mother, Lebanese father, Lakota grandfather, a life on the margins of
mainstream and Indian, somewhere in between American respectabilities and
Native American closures Paula Gunn Allen writes in the shadows of visions,
"fingering silence and sound" with a poet's touching measure. She sings desire,
need, grief, confusion, and rage over a horizon note of loss. *Shadow Country:*
that marginal zone of interfusions, neither the shadower nor the shadowed,
both and neither, in liminal transition.

In the halfway house of mixed ancestry, Paula Allen does not so much live
in a tribe as try to articulate her sense of the tribal and still live, without rhetorical claims, choosing Native American definitions, defining Native America in
her life. Allen knows only too well the tribal sense of alienation, the corre-
sponding necessity for mutual assimilations, America and Native America.

Rediscovering traditional Indian ways, Paula Allen also records new adaptations, shattering old stereotypes of blood warriors and demure squaws,
reconstituting new images of real people from the Indian debris. Her poems
voice the polychromatic shock of Indian modernism, in Fritz Scholder's paintings, for example, where cowboy Indians slouch with cigarettes and dark
glasses, Coors beer and American flag shawls, ice cream and umbrellas on
horses.

With a girl-child's sensitivity to pain, Allen is concerned with a woman's
self-images and self-esteems. Men stand in the distances, women fore-
grounded. In "Off Reservation Blues" she dreams the Lady of Laguna, locked
in a tower of defeated fantasy, earth-fearing, behind glass and above a white-
skinned figure who waves but cannot hear:

> night was coming
> and I had to speak
> raise my hand and hit the glass
> I groaned
> sound too soft to hear

The grief language of her mute body registers speechless acts. She braves see-through barriers of sex, race, class, education, language, "civilization," consciousness itself in its many definitions—out of that breed no (wo)man's land of pained inarticulations, potentially revolutionary on the poet's tongue. Existing wholly in neither Indian nor non-Indian classifications, she assimilates both as best she can. 〈. . .〉

Paula Allen writes with the complete and myriad sensitivities of a woman with children, with a husband; in love, out of love; married, divorced, redefined: old women with weavings and potteries, new women with separations and new definitions. "No you can't use me," an Indian mother defies abuse,

> but you can share
> me with me as though
> I were a two-necked wedding jar
> they make, over in Santa Clara—
> some for each of us
> enough ("Indian Mother Poem")

Often, a woman's teasing opacity tints the poems, refusing linear logics and singular openings, in search of shared questions that place the poet, many-minded and multiply emotional, among her literary shadows (echoes of Whitman and his descendents Pound, Williams, Olson, Creeley, Snyder).

—Kenneth Lincoln, "Native American Literatures: 'old like hills, like stars,'" in *Three American Literatures: Essays in Chicano, Native American, and Asian-American Literature for Teachers of American Literature*, ed. Houston A. Baker, Jr. (New York: The Modern Language Association of America, 1982), 137–38, 140

ELAINE JAHNER

The way in which Allen balances the diverse elements of her heritage with her own voracious inquiry into all systems of human thought—religious, philosophical, and political—is well illustrated in *Coyote's Daylight Trip*. At a first reading the poems seem unconnected to each other, but a careful study of the book's major themes reveals a process of learning documented by the various poems. At first we find nostalgic idealism and longing for the kind of community the poet intuitively believes once to have been in existence at Laguna Pueblo. Then comes a realization that she must identify with contemporary fragmentation and loss. With identification comes the possibility for transformation of the pain found in urban streets, and finally the poet knows she is creating not only poems but the actual patterns for a new way of life.

The entire process implies a belief in the mythic foundations of metaphor and poetry giving language what N. Scott Momaday has called "its deeper and more vital context" than is usually taken into account ⟨in *Carriers of the Dream Wheel*, ed. Duane Niatum, 1975, xx⟩. Poetry that so directly relates to myth is written in order to function as myth does in society, establishing structures (or metaphors) that not only make the world intelligible and help people see it in a new way but also teach people about the creative powers of the universe. Belief in these powers is part of the religious tradition of all tribes. Creating poetry that is a contemporary realization of the powers of mythic processes is a quite different matter from merely using myth as a source of imagery or allusions. While the content of specific poems may reflect specific American Indian myths, a poem does not have to include overt reference to anything Native American to show how the energies dramatized in ancient myths can still shape life in today's city streets. Following through her book Paula Gunn Allen's vision of how myths function today can be for the reader a remarkable experience of seeing previously unimagined facets of American life. ⟨. . .⟩

The various strands of meaning at work in *Coyote's Daylight Trip* come together when we realize that it is in mythic space that one can be truly at home. By the end of the book there is an answer to the early cry: "I would go home, crazy old woman, if I knew where that might be, or how." The poet has found her way home by freeing herself of nostalgic dreams about finding a place where life could be lived as it once was. Then she had to identify with her own urban existence even though that meant the pain of loss and disorientation amidst a culture that glorifies the illusory. With identification came recognition of possibilities for turning what is illusory into metaphors that link the present with mythic patterns, thus making artistic expression of contemporary life into the prophetic continuation of myth. Poetry is not just passive description. It points toward appropriate action.

—Elaine Jahner, "A Laddered, Rain-bearing Rug: Paula Gunn Allen's Poetry," in *Women and Western American Literature*, ed. Helen Winter Stauffer and Susan J. Rosowski (Troy, NY: The Whitson Publishing Company, 1982), 312–13, 323

FRANCHOT BALLINGER AND BRIAN SWANN
⟨Interview with Paula Gunn Allen by Franchot Ballinger and Brian Swann⟩

PGA: ⟨. . .⟩ The Lagunas are a heavily "mother right" culture. I won't call it matriarchal, because that means something real bizarre in English, that no Indian ever dreamed of, believe me. But nevertheless, they're woman-dominant; they're woman-centered people, and that's important to my work.

FB/BS: Can ⟨we⟩ ask an obvious question? Given your background and your culture and the way in which you straddle cultures or have incorporated a number of cultures, what makes an Indian?

PGA: I believe that it's a turn of mind. I don't speak Laguna, and I find myself in enormous trouble continually. It's a trouble I didn't understand until *House Made of Dawn* came out. There was no way to understand it. But it seems to me that what happens is that I think like a Laguna. But I have only English to talk in, and so I'm saying that it's a consciousness style more than a cultural style. ⟨. . .⟩

⟨. . . You⟩ learn what your language means by the subtle signals—behavioral, and inflectionary and environmental—signals that you get from your primary raisers: i.e., my mother and my grandmother, who lived right next door. So I was raised by Laguna women. They spoke English, but they never mean the same thing, like they say something that has a particular meaning to them that is different from the general sense of what the same words mean but their associations and understandings and expectations about a statement are very, very different. Their understanding of the world is conditioned by their Laguna culture. They speak a very interesting language; they speak something I suspect is a half-breed language, and that is common to half-breeds all over the country, regardless of what tribes they come from. And I don't understand that clearly; it's something that I don't have the expertise to be able to explore, except in my own work. I can do it as a poet and a storyteller, but as a scholar I simply don't have the background.

FB/BS: Has anybody done a study on this? Like Black English?

PGA: No, but we do have an English. I notice it in my students continually. I can spot an Indian writer, and I notice it in the critics. Every time I get a paper from an Indian scholar to read, I *know* that an Indian wrote it, and I *know* when an Indian didn't write it (or had it thoroughly edited). And what it is, is structure. It's not sentence structure so much as it is thought structure. We have a habit of inverting the introductory paragraphs into the center of the paper. We have a habit of talking, what looks like "talking around in circles"; actually, we structure thought in accretive bursts. The clearest example of this I can think of is Momaday's "Man Made of Words." If you follow that article, if you understand what I'm saying, you can plot it. If you don't understand what I'm saying, you can't make any sense out of the article. It's very hard to follow, if you want a linearly developed argument. But if you let him just meander through your mind, as he tells a story, tells a joke—all of it finally begins to point in the same direction, toward the ultimate significance of his utterance. But you can't analyze it in the way you could an ordinary piece of essay writing. We all do it.

—Franchot Ballinger and Brian Swann, "A MELUS Interview: Paula Gunn Allen," *MELUS* 10, no. 2 (Summer 1983): 6–7

ANNIE O. EYSTUROY

⟨Interview with Paula Gunn Allen by Annie O. Eysturoy⟩

AOE: It seems to me that in *The Woman Who Owned the Shadows*, Ephanie, the central character, is on a vision quest. On that quest she moves further and further into a female universe, while the male characters are basically negative characters. How do you achieve the balance there that—as we have talked about—is so important in American Indian philosophy, the balance of male and female? How does Ephanie reach that balance?

PGA: She reaches it because in a woman's life femininity is central; in a man's life masculinity is central. You don't get egalitarianism by women relating to men and you don't get it by men relating to women. What I am saying is that gender norms are for the gender to which they apply; they are not for the other gender. For Ephanie to locate who she is, she has to move from thinking of her reference group as male to thinking of her reference group as female. That says nothing about the men. Ephanie herself is pretty crazy—out of touch with herself—until she understands that she is female.

AOE: So she has to move into a female universe in order to explore herself?

PGA: A truly female universe.

AOE: . . . from which she can emerge and be her true self, and then unite with her male counterpart?

PGA: Or not. Uniting is one of the things white people do. There is a male and there is a female. There is not a "unite" in there anywhere, and there never is in the tribes. And why should they unite? They are different.

AOE: So they should operate in their separate spheres with balance between those spheres?

PGA: That's right. Yes, and with mutual respect. You know, if you look at the plain we are on, you see the Sandias, which I have always thought of as male, and across, way across, is Mt. Taylor, whom I always have thought of as female. She stays there, and he stays here and they converse. They don't get mixed up in thinking that one has to be the other one, and they don't think they have to merge. If they ever do think that, we are in trouble, all of us who live in between. And that's why the mountains are that way, and that's how I see the appropriate balance of genders. I think that we live in separate spheres. We have different consciousnesses, because we have different bodies. We need each other; but only if we recognize the validity of our own way, and therefore the validity of the other person's way, are we ever going to be able to actually function together.

AOE: We should accept the differences?

PGA: Absolutely, and use them; it is essential. You know, patriarchy is about monogamy, it is about monotony, it is about monotheism, it is about unity, and it is about uniformity. No Indian system is like that, in any sense. They never wanted other people to be like them. That's why they don't recruit members. They don't only respect difference and acknowledge it; they expect it, and they always have. That's why they got conquered, as a matter of fact. They did not understand that there were people who thought that there was only one way of doing things and that was their way, and if you did not do it their way they would kill you.

Ephanie, in *The Woman Who Owned the Shadows*, is not supposed to unite with the men. She keeps expecting men to do her life for her, because she got feminized in the western way instead of the tribal way. She made a terrible mistake and she paid for it until she understood that she had power in her own right.

—Annie O. Eysturoy, [Interview with Paula Gunn Allen], in *This Is About Vision: Interviews with Southwestern Writers*, ed. William Balassi, John F. Crawford, and Annie O. Eysturoy (Albuquerque: University of New Mexico Press, 1990), 102–3

ANNETTE VAN DYKE

Allen's novel, *The Woman Who Owned the Shadows*, is about a journey to healing—a journey back to the female center. At the beginning of the novel, the central character, Ephanie Atencio, is a half-breed who has lost the sense of who she is; she is isolated and fragmented as a human being, belonging neither to the pueblo community nor to the non-Indian community. Ephanie has a fragmented self from an inner war. As a half-breed Guadalupe woman, Ephanie is caught in the erosion of the traditional place of honor and respect in which a Guadalupe woman is held by her tribe and in the stereotyped and patriarchal view from which she is viewed by non-Indians. She is surrounded by forces which work to destroy whatever link she has to the traditional culture in which the women were central figures. The reader follows her struggle to regain her sanity as she sorts out her childhood and her tribal beliefs and connections, marries a second-generation Japanese-American man, and deals with the death of one of their twins. She joins a consciousness-raising group, goes to a psychiatrist, studies the old traditions, and tries to commit suicide, but it is only when she is able to synthesize what she has learned from all of this, see its connection to her tribal traditions, and reaffirm the importance of the female, especially the importance of the "amazon tradition" ⟨Walter L. Williams, *The Spirit and the Flesh*, 1986, 11⟩, that she is healed. ⟨. . .⟩

By allowing the reader to participate in the curing ceremony of the novel by following the main character in her own restoration of balance, Allen seeks to restore balance to the community-at-large. Through this the reader is reminded of the power of storytelling and the responsibility of each human to the community. Further, if, as Judy Grahn says in her comment on the back cover, "you come with an honest heart," the novel enables the non-Indian reader to begin to see from a non-Euro-American perspective. To begin to change the Euro-American vision of disconnectedness to one of connectedness would be a "curing" indeed. As Williams notes, a most important function of a curing is a "healing of the mind" (34). Although the novel ends with Ephanie's understanding of her connection to her heritage and although the reader does not see how it will affect her life, Allen's novel is also an important offering to Native American lesbians. She has shown a connection that present-day lesbians might make to a special spiritual heritage and role which such women played in Native American cultures. As Allen says, "It all has to do with spirit, with restoring an awareness of our spirituality as gay people" (quoted in Williams 251).

More generally in the novel, the healing of the main character occurs when she is able to reconnect with the female principle which is exemplified in Thought Woman and her sisters and consists particularly of life and strength—she recovers the ancient qualities of woman who was seen as "strong and powerful," balancing the ancient qualities of man who was seen as having "transient or transitory" qualities (Allen, "Where I Come From" 17). This balancing of qualities where "woman-ness is not of less value than man-ness" (17) allows both the individual and tribe to continue and prosper. The telling of the story allows the listeners/readers to visualize how their experiences fit into the great web of being, the patterns of life. The story and the experiences become one, leading to harmony and healing.

—Annette Van Dyke, "The Journey Back to Female Roots: A Laguna Pueblo Model," in *Lesbian Texts and Contexts: Radical Revisions*, ed. Karla Jay and Joanne Glasgow (New York: New York University Press, 1990), 342, 351

HELEN JASKOSKI

⟨In "Grandmother"⟩ it is tempting to assume ⟨. . .⟩ that the speaker is a woman. The speaker of "Grandmother," however, is emphatically ungendered or androgynous. Grandmother Spider, female Great Mother, is the archetypal progenitor for weavers, who ⟨in Pueblo culture⟩ were traditionally male. Now, according to the poem, a further evolution in the process of creation sees both women and men as weavers, storytellers, and builders of the houses of memory. The poem's speaker takes the place of the Grandmother who "disappeared" after completing her work of creation; the speaker sits on the blanket (creation) to "mend the tear" in it—an activity that may be read as reweaving the gap caused by both the disappearance of grandmother/creator and the erasure of women from the creative activities of weaving and storytelling. The woven blanket is itself a figure of androgyny, composed of warp and weft, in which neither can predominate and both must be literally interlocked.

The complex of spider-weaver-poet and the blanket as metaphor for androgyny also makes this poem a bridge that connects Euroamerican and American Indian poetic traditions through its echoes of two other works. In "A Noiseless Patient Spider," Whitman, preeminent celebrator of the androgynous self in American literature, also parallels the creations of spider and poet. On the other hand, the blanket as a figure of androgyny is the core metaphor in a traditional Pueblo poem collected by Spinden: The Tewa "Song of the Sky Loom" opens and closes with invocations to Mother Earth and Father Sky; the body of the poem parallels warp and weft with white light and red light, dawn and sunset, falling rain and standing rainbow. In traditional Pueblo and other southwestern cultures, each of these natural elements—rain, light, and so on—is gendered, so that the blanket, itself an image of the coming rainstorm, metaphorically weaves together into a seamless whole the balancing opposites of male and female.

—Helen Jaskoski, "Allen's 'Grandmother,'" *The Explicator* 50, no. 4 (Summer 1992): 248–49

B I B L I O G R A P H Y

The Blind Lion. 1974.

Coyote's Daylight Trip. 1978.

A Cannon between My Knees. 1981.

From the Center: A Folio, Native American Art and Poetry (editor). 1981.

Star Child. 1981.

Shadow Country. 1982.

The Woman Who Owned the Shadows. 1983.

Studies in American Indian Literature: Critical Essays and Course Designs (editor). 1983.

Wyrds. 1987.

Skin and Bones: Poems 1979–87. 1988.

Spider Woman's Granddaughters (editor). 1989.

Grandmothers of the Light: A Medicine Woman's Sourcebook. 1991.

The Sacred Hoop (editor). 1992.

Voice of the Turtle: American Indian Literature 1900–1970 (editor). 1994.

As Long As the Rivers Flow: The Stories of Nine Native Americans (editor, with Patricia Clark Smith). 1996.

Life Is a Fatal Disease: Selected Poems 1964–1994. 1996.

Song of the Turtle: American Indian Literature 1974–1994 (editor). 1996.

MARIA CAMPBELL

B. 1940

MARIA CAMPBELL was born in 1940 in northern Saskatchewan. A Canadian Métis, or mixed-blood, she was shunned by both full-blooded Indians and by the white community. Her mother died when Maria was only 12, and in an attempt to save her six younger siblings from being placed in an orphanage, Maria herself married at 15. Her husband, however, reported her to the authorities, and her siblings were removed from her care. From this point, her life deteriorated even further: her husband, an alcoholic, deserted her, and she turned to drugs and prostitution. After joining Alcoholics Anonymous, Campbell says she started writing so she would have someone to talk to.

Campbell's first and best-known book, *Halfbreed* (1973), unflinchingly records the discrimination and racism to which the Métis have historically been subjected. Providing a personal account of the Métis' political situation in Canada, the book also portrays Campbell's search for self-identity, her descent into and recovery from prostitution and drug addiction, and her love for her great-grandmother, Cheechum, who helped her survive. From Cheechum, Campbell says, she learned that the community can be a source of power; remembering Cheechum's stories helped her to discard the negative images assigned to Métis women. *Halfbreed* has been described as a combination of sociology, ethnography, political tract, and personal narrative; it is sometimes seen as following in the tradition of such 19th-century Native American writers as Sarah Winnemucca.

Campbell adapted *Halfbreed* for the stage under the title *Jessica* (1982) in collaboration with non-Native actress and playwright Linda Griffiths. The two women attempted to collaborate on a nonfiction project, *The Book of Jessica* (1989), as a way to narrate their respective difficulties in bringing the play to the stage. However, the writing relationship was fraught with further difficulty, due in part to the cultural and political differences between Griffiths and Campbell. *The Book of Jessica* is considered by many to be a testament, in a context of collaboration, to the problems of cross-cultural appropriation and colonization.

In addition to her autobiographical writings, Campbell is known for her political work and her writing for children, such as *People of the Buffalo* (1976), and *Riel's People* (1977), both of which relate Métis traditions and history. In all her work, Campbell says that she is trying to create and encourage a dialogue between people of different ethnic groups that will be meaningful and honest and that will perhaps ultimately lead to political and social change.

CRITICAL EXTRACTS

GRETCHEN M. BATAILLE AND KATHLEEN M. SANDS

There is a circular pattern to Maria Campbell's autobiography, for it begins with her return to her childhood home. The description in the Introduction is one of desolation and of emptiness; there is little left of the physical past ⟨. . . .⟩

Seventeen years have passed, and Maria Campbell has returned home; but what of those seventeen years and what of the years before that, the years she spent growing up on this land? She tells in the Introduction why she is writing her autobiography: "I write this for all of you, to tell you what it is like to be a Halfbreed woman in our country. I want to tell you about the joys and sorrows, the oppressing poverty, the frustrations and the dreams" ⟨Halfbreed, 8⟩.

To fulfill that purpose she must go back and record the realities and the dreams of her childhood. Her autobiography is the culmination of her personal search: "If I was to know peace I would have to search within myself," she writes ⟨7–8⟩.

Maria Campbell's life story is one of poverty, of deprivation, of alcoholism and prostitution, and finally it is a story of the strength in knowing who she is. Through her search she came to understand the message her great-grandmother Cheechum had been trying to communicate. The autobiography of Maria Campbell is clearly a product of contemporary experience. It is frank, and the pain of Campbell's life comes through clearly. The events of her life might be unique, except that the status of Indian people in Canada has been well documented, particularly the deplorable conditions of the Métis, or Halfbreeds, who do not have treaty rights with the government. Maria Campbell is a Halfbreed, and she is only too aware of what that means in her country.

The arbitrary labels of *Halfbreed, Métis, Indian, status Indian, nonstatus Indian,* and *Eskimo* continue to work their evil, just as Cheechum told her granddaughter they would: "The white man saw that that was a more powerful weapon than anything else with which to beat the Halfbreeds, and he used it and still does today. Already they are using it on you. They try to make you hate your people" ⟨47⟩. Conflict among the groups is inflamed by the different ways in which they are treated by the government and the Indian Act of 1951. Labels are legal in nature and do not reflect blood quantum, parentage, or cultural identification. An Indian woman loses her Indian status if she marries a white; a white woman can gain Indian status and a place on the reserve if she marries an Indian. Indian men do not face the same restrictions, adding another internal conflict.

Although Campbell's book is written as autobiography, it incorporates urban and rural sociology, a study of ethnic relations in Canada, and a historical account of the political situation; but primarily it is literature. She is aware of the need to develop her plot, to use suspense, and to end the narrative neatly when the protagonist is about to set out on a new and more promising venture. Having experienced the most negative aspects of life, she has rehabilitated herself, has written the story of her life up to that point, and has ended the narrative on a note of resolution and promise that allows us to speculate on her future.

Central to Campbell's development of her personal search for identity is the character of Cheechum, a guiding force in the narrator's life and a unifying force in the narrative structure of the text. It is the advice and counsel of this woman, old already when we meet her, that is important. When Campbell writes of her integration into the family and community, she says: "As far back as I can remember Daddy taught me how to set traps, shoot a rifle, and fight like a boy. Mom did her best to turn me into a lady, showing me how to cook, sew and knit, while Cheechum, my best friend and confidante, tried to teach me all she knew about living" ⟨19⟩.

When Cheechum dies in an accident at the age of 104, Campbell has reached a climax in her life. Will Cheechum's advice have been in vain, or will Campbell finally understand it? The story is dramatic and moving. Her Cree great-grandmother has been very important, and now that Campbell must make some crucial decisions, she will have to follow the advice of the wise old woman. Cheechum, then, is a literary device, although no less real for that fact, and she serves to direct the thoughts and actions of the narrator as she develops her story, which she tells deliberately and, at times, quite self-consciously.

—Gretchen M. Bataille and Kathleen M. Sands, *American Indian Women Telling Their Lives* (Lincoln: University of Nebraska Press, 1984), 118–20

HELEN M. BUSS

The struggle to become strong despite the deprivation of an important maternal element in childhood marks the life of Maria Campbell, the author of *Halfbreed* (1973; 157 pp.); the effort is complicated not only by poverty, but by her position at the bottom of everyone's social scale, that of a mixed-blood person. It is a typical move of one desiring "connection" to give her autobiography the same name as has been used as a term of scorn for mixed-blood people by both whites and Indians in Canadian society. Instead of separating herself from the term of abuse, she transforms it into a term of pride, just as she transformed her own life from degradation, to one of political action and pride.

Like other achieving women, she starts life as her father's favorite. Until a younger brother grows old enough, she is the one who accompanies her father hunting and engages in other father-son activities. Her identification with him seems to be part of the cause of her later abuse of her female body. Her father, though often generous and loving, beats and abuses her mother in response to his own frustrations as a halfbreed persecuted by white society. The death of her mother (from illness aggravated by poverty and abuse) when Campbell is still a child leaves the daughter prematurely responsible for herself and others. Later in life, Campbell not only subjects herself to the exploitation of men, but exploits her own body through prostitution, as well as through alcohol and drug abuse. Just as her father abused her mother, she, taking her father as her role model, abuses the female in herself.

The autobiography becomes a powerful confessional instrument which Campbell uses to put her own degradation behind her. It is also a means to help other aboriginal people. Through the detailing of her own pain and accomplishment she shows how such a renewal can be gained. At this point of renewal, when she is attempting to restructure her personality in a less self-destructive mode, she finds she cannot do so without reference to strong maternal models. Another mixed-blood woman "mothers" her and helps her to return to the model that has always been available in Campbell's life, but not realized until she undertakes a conscious journey towards self-transformation. Campbell's paternal great-grandmother, "Cheechum," was a mixed-blood woman who was a niece of Gabriel Dumont (the fighting lieutenant who led Riel's forces). She never swerved in her loyalties to Riel and the Metis desire for a homeland of their own in her long and difficult life in which she had to fight not only the prejudices of whites, but also the treatment inflicted by mixed-blood men on their women. In her dealings with Campbell she emphasized pride in herself as a mixed-blood person and as a woman. It was Cheechum who had once told Campbell that she would have to go out into

the world and find her own answers. Near the end of *Halfbreed* Campbell realizes that she has "misinterpreted what she [Cheechum] had taught me. She
had never meant that I should go out into the world in search of fortune, but
rather that I go out and discover for myself the need for leadership and
change" (143). In other words, the ego-shaped journey for individual "fortune"
is not suitable for a mixed-blood woman; hers must be a journey towards "leadership," towards relationship.

For Campbell that has meant a strong political involvement in the
progress of her people, one often hampered by the attitudes of men inside her
community. But she takes an insightful feminist posture on this matter: "I've
met many native leaders who have treated me the same [as an inferior because
she is female] and I've learned to accept it. I realize now that the system that
fucked me up fucked up our men even worse. The missionaries had impressed
upon us the feeling that women were a source of evil. This belief, combined
with the ancient Indian recognition of the power of women, is still holding
back the progress of our people today" (144).

Through her use of Cheechum as a paradigm, and through the writing of
her autobiography, Campbell attempts to restore an archetypal image of
woman as powerful and good. The importance of this concept as the implicit
intention of *Halfbreed* is emphasized by the way in which she traces her own
fall from innocence to an "evil" life and her restoration of herself to a position
of "good" woman, as both mother and political activist. Her final emphasis on
the importance of the strong and good woman as archetypal leader for Native
people is made by ending the autobiography with the death of Cheechum,
who "waited all her life for a new generation of people who would make this
country a better place to live in" (156). By implication Campbell sees herself
as a leader of that "new generation," in the way that Cheechum once predicted
she would be.

—Helen M. Buss, "The Different Voice of Canadian Feminist Autobiographers," *Biography:
An Interdisciplinary Quarterly* 13, no. 2 (Spring 1990): 165–66

HARTMUT LUTZ
⟨Interview with Maria Campbell by Hartmut Lutz and Konrad Gross, 1989⟩

MC: Each time I wrote a book, it *had* to come, there had to be a reason why I
was writing it. The two books that I wrote for children, I wrote for my children, because they were at school, and there was no material for them.

The last book that I wrote, *Little Badger and Fire Spirit*, was written because
my grandson wanted to know where we got fire.

After that I couldn't write. I tried and tried, I mean I had lots that I wanted to say, but when I put it down on paper it sounded as if I was lecturing. There was something missing. And I went around for four, five years, really frustrated. I could articulate it, but it had no spirit in it! I blamed the English language, because I felt that the language was manipulating me.

So I went to the old man who's been my mentor, my teacher, my grandfather, whatever you want to call him. It was the first time I'd ever talked to him about the struggle I had. I had talked to him about storytelling, but I never talked to him about what I felt the language was doing to me; going to him as a writer to another writer.

And he just laughed, probably thinking, "Why didn't she come here a long time ago!" "It's really simple," he said, "why you have trouble with the English language, it's because the language has no Mother. This language lost its Mother a long time ago, and what you have to do is, put the Mother back in the language!"

And then I went away, and I thought, "Now, how am I going to put the Mother back in the language?" Because, in our language, and in our culture, as well as Indian people's culture, Mother is the land.

So I tried, but what I ended up sounding like was an evangelist minister. Talking about the Mother, the Mother, constantly. So that still didn't do it.

And then, one day, my dad came to stay with me for a weekend. And my father is always telling me something. He'll be making something, and then he'll say, "You know, I just remembered." He has an association, and it reminds him of something. So he told me a story and I listened to him that night. I woke up about two o'clock in the morning. I had this most incredible inspiration that I had something I wanted to say. So, I went to the typewriter, and I started working. This was the first time that I've been struck with total inspiration—when they say "the muses," I call it "Grandmothers" coming. I really know what that means. I worked about five hours, and it felt like an hour.

I had the story in my father's voice, or somebody's voice. It was all there. I could smell the community, I could smell the old people, all those familiar things were there. And what I had been trying to say, over and over again, in rewriting and everything else, I said in this broken English. And it was eloquent, it was full of humour, it was full of love, and yet it was hard. It was all there. And that was when I understood what the old man said about the Mother in the language.

My father is very close to the land. If you asked him about Mother Earth he wouldn't know how to answer you, because he doesn't know how to say it. But he lives off the land, he's been a hunter and trapper all his life. He respects the land. He's one of those old people who puts tobacco out before he goes out in the morning, sings his song in the morning. But if I asked my father,

"What's our culture?" he'd say, "We don't have one," because he doesn't know what "culture" means. And he wouldn't understand if I tried to explain it to him. ⟨. . .⟩

⟨. . .⟩ When I'd say, "Dad, don't we have any stories? I mean, don't we have any stories about culture?" Even when I said it in his language, he'd say "No, I don't know any!" I've been deaf to him. All these years he had been telling me stories, but I was expecting something profound.

You see what happened to me was that I was thinking English. It's really hard to explain what that is. So now I have the old man's voice. Sometimes, when I am doing a story, or sometimes when I'm doing a poem, I think, "I'll write it in English, the way I talk." But I can't get it. And then all of a sudden I'll start to type. And the poem will come, I almost never have to rewrite, because it all comes. And sometimes it's just saying something in real broken English, like, "Boy, you know, that man, he talks to the eagles, too." That will say what I would spend an hour and 10 pages trying to explain, just saying that man looks like he talks to eagles, that will tell everything.

But I can't control it. This voice is really inspired. And it doesn't, he doesn't, always want to come. I'll think "Gee, this will make a good story, me sitting, having dinner with these people who are German, and I am exchanging this. I'm going to go home, and I am going to write it in the old man's voice." There is no way! He won't come in! He decides what he is going to talk about, and I can't manipulate him at all. And he's a man, but his voice is the Mother.

I have another voice, that's the old lady. But the old lady is very masculine. She tells the men's stories. I can't get her to tell the women's stories, and I can't get him to tell the men's stories! So it's like opposites, the contrary, or whatever. So I don't question it any more! I just know it works.

—Hartmut Lutz, *Contemporary Challenges: Conversations with Canadian Native Authors* (Saskatoon, SK: Fifth House Publishers, 1991), 48–50

Helen M. Buss

Part of the patriarchal nature of the world ⟨Campbell⟩ enters as an adult is a set of generic imperatives in which language, itself patriarchally constructed, allows insufficient generic forms (such as confession, apologia, essay, memoir) for the inscription of a female subjectivity. Campbell is as much victim of this insufficiency in telling her story as are other women. The force of generic convention makes her nostalgic about a childhood that was anything but a good preparation for life as a female. Still, she adopts this nostalgic position because she wishes to express the positive in her heritage; however, our writing tradition offers her only the gloss of nostalgia, a gloss that hides the terrible economic and social conditions under which Campbell lived. In the same way, she falls into a confessional and romantic mode in which she is the sinner rather than the victim and too often seeks to be the maiden rescued by a hero. Ironically, Campbell sometimes gives credit for her "conversion" to her identification with a cause (like the spiritual autobiographer in the European tradition, identification with a religion), thus disguising the record of her own growth in womanhood through the help of female surrogate mothers and her own imaginative efforts. It is difficult to estimate the effect of the mandate a writer receives in the personal world where friends, relatives, and cultural allies wish her to represent only a portion of the reality of their shared past, but at the very beginning of the account she reproduces a conversation with a friend who asks her to make her book a "happy book" ⟨Halfbreed, 13⟩. This is perhaps our warning, and our permission, to read Campbell's account in the larger context of other women's accounts and through facilitating theories of female development, since sometimes the effort to make the book happy leads Campbell to elide important aspects of her identity as a woman.

However, these textual slants may not be entirely Campbell's doing, since she has admitted that Halfbreed was a much longer book before the editors at McClelland and Stewart began to shape it to marketable length and form. Yet somewhere in the bridging of these male lifewriting forms, and perhaps despite her editors, she is able to inscribe the trace of an alternate subjectivity, one rhythmed by her paradigm of Cheechum and her own place as mother and female community worker, one that can be maximized by a feminist reading for female subjectivity and genre transgression and bridging.

—Helen M. Buss, *Mapping Our Selves: Canadian Women's Autobiography in English* (Montreal: McGill-Queen's University Press, 1993), 144

HELEN HOY

However well-intentioned, *The Book of Jessica* redeploys the strategies of intellectual colonialism. Originally conceived as a full collaboration, it has by the time of publication fallen back under Griffiths' editorial control. So it replicates the originary Native Informant/Master Discourse model of the play itself. (According to Diane Bessai, early programme notes for *Jessica* credited Campbell with the subject matter, Griffiths and director Paul Thompson with the dialogue and structure respectively [104]). Campbell's decision to run as President of the Métis Society of Saskatchewan and withdraw from the collaborative project, a decision only tersely acknowledged in the introductory "History"—and unglossed—speaks loudly in the vacuum created by her editorial absence. As a final refusal/indifference/signal of divided allegiance, an eloquently silent codicil to the text that resonates with earlier repudiations, it pushes against the reconciliatory drift of the narrative. Unrancorous post-publication interviews by Campbell ⟨. . .⟩ mute the contestatory impact of her defection, in that arena, but the decision functions as a disruption *textually* at least.

It is Griffiths, then, who provides the framing narrative—tellingly referring to herself three times in the opening line alone—and who selects both her own and Campbell's words, in what nevertheless purports to be a dialogue. Just as the programme credits for *Jessica* shift between 1981 and 1986 from three co-authors to "Written by: Linda Griffiths, in collaboration with Maria Campbell" (116), so the hierarchy of authorship for *The Book of Jessica*—Griffiths followed by Campbell—gives precedence to the one-time final formal setting-down-on-paper, to the value of individually exercised verbal and structural creativity and control. What has happened to Maria's gift of "her life, her philosophy and entry to her deepest self" (48)? But, in one sense, that arrogation of pre-eminence on the title page speaks true. Given the editorial process, this story can now finally only be read as Griffiths'. ⟨. . .⟩

⟨However⟩ *The Book of Jessica* is Maria Campbell's book. It is her idea initially. The very substance and format of the book are determined by her ethos of mutual self-disclosure as fundamental to any true collaboration. Provoked by the inconsistency of Griffiths' fascination exclusively with a Native past, arguing that she and Griffiths can find a meeting place only in an *exchange* of their ancestral histories, and contending that shared personal matters, like Griffiths' shoplifting, give her someone solid to interact with, she ensures that this text both theorizes and models a collaborative process of genuine exchange. Though deletions leave their traces—Griffiths' mother's alcoholism(?) cured through religion, for example—Griffiths is exposed in ways foreign to sibyls and researchers. The textual format of dialogue and interjections, in place of a monologic or synthesized narrative, develops naturally from this insistence on mutuality. The book's forthrightness too reflects Campbell's motive for persisting with a project this painful, the urgency of providing connections and hope in a period of global devastation.

Furthermore, the most eloquent piece of oratory in the book is Campbell's. In its historic concision and controlled passion, it necessarily infuses any reading of the entire collaboration and the book. The speech I mean is her caustic response to Griffiths' contention that the play *Jessica* lives thanks to Griffiths' authorship but requires Campbell's belated modifications and permission:

> Now Wolverine is saying, "I took it. I gave it birth. I gave it life. It
> was mine and it would have died without me. I salvaged it. I built
> temples all over the place. I built high-rises all over the place. I put

wheat fields out there. I produced it and if it wasn't for me, you would have let this land die. So I came along and I took what you were wasting and I made something productive out of it, because you weren't doing it, but I need you to tell me that I didn't steal anything, that I didn't take anything from you." (80)

Campbell inserts the narrative so forcibly and repeatedly into history, and into a colonial history, that the reader cannot help but read the collaboration as one moment in a centuries-long struggle.

—Helen Hoy, "'When You Admit You're a Thief, Then You Can Be Honourable': Native/Non-Native Collaboration in *The Book of Jessica,*" *Canadian Literature* 136 (Spring 1993): 26, 34–35

Susanna Egan

Theatre was a natural choice for the author of *Halfbreed* precisely because it works as live performance and blurs the boundaries between contingent reality and its narrative interpretation. "Theatre . . . gives the oral tradition a three-dimensional context," Tomson Highway explains, "telling stories by using actors and the visual aspect of the stage" ⟨Penny Petrone, *Native Literature in Canada,* 1990, 173⟩. It provided one more way in which Campbell could extend the story she needed to tell beyond the limitations of the printed word and ensure its return to the community. This particular theatrical drama, furthermore, enacts the drama with which we began—about who may speak and who may listen and what the listener may do with what she hears. Drama can work as process—back into the past and forward into political effect. It contains revolutionary potential; you speak and I listen and play back what I have heard; in *The Book of Jessica,* such exchanges involve rage and silence and magnificent instances of hard-won empathy. The dialogue/drama continues and diminishes its own possibility of closure.

For this Métis woman, furthermore, the performance of relationship, the intersubjectivity with a white woman, becomes performatively significant for the autobiographical act. For her, as Jessica, and as Maria-and-Linda, the woman-self is not singular but interactive, mediating and mediated. And this mediation, that is performed agonistically by two women of each other, sets up a cyclical motion. "This mind goes in circles," says the grandmother-figure of Vitaline in the play. "[A]nd don't you forget it" (167). Her circles are those of the grandmothers, of the spirit world, of prayers for protection, of relationships in process, of recognition that all life forms are connected and responsible to each other, of performance that contains but does not confine evolution of character and of life story. Both the play and its dramatic context connect the inner life with its outer appearance in repeated transformations so

that these women are both mother and daughter, both hurting and healing, both present and absent as befits the best of autobiographers—readers, writers, and performers for each other.
   —Susanna Egan, "*The Book of Jessica*: The Healing Circle of a Woman's Autobiography," *Canadian Literature* 144 (Spring 1995): 22–23

JODI LUNGREN

Campbell ⟨. . .⟩ uses the form of autobiography to subvert the master narrative of white imperialist history. Using conciseness as a form of understatement, Campbell, in a few pages at the beginning of ⟨*Halfbreed*⟩, recounts critical events for the Metis in the nineteenth and early twentieth centuries and eloquently demonstrates the impact of colonization and racism on her people. She reveals the way in which impossible circumstances produced in the Metis feelings of failure and shame which have been passed down intergenerationally. She explodes the image of lazy, dirty Halfbreeds promulgated by white sources (3–9). Campbell modestly undercuts this exposition by saying, "But I am ahead of myself" (9), as though this causal analysis had been a mere digression, an error in chronology. It is precisely this sort of interruption of linear history which makes *Halfbreed* an act of decolonization. As Barbara Godard says:

> Narrative is a way of exploring history and questioning the historical narratives of the colonizer which have violently interposed themselves in place of the history of the colonized. Experimentation, especially with structures of chronology, is part of this challenge, a radical questioning of historiographical versions of the past as developed in the "master narratives," in order to rewrite the historical ending.
> ⟨"The Politics of Representation," 1990, 198⟩

Conventional linear history would tend to flatten out Campbell's comprehensive analysis under the strictures of chronological order. Indeed, *Halfbreed* was subjected to "the reshaping activities of an editor" (Godard 225, n.49) in order to make it "fit the conventions of Native life-writing" (Godard 204). Fortunately, some of Campbell's subversive strategies slipped past the editor.
    Campbell disregards chronology again when she gives a preview of her childhood games at the end of Chapter Two before recording her own birth at the beginning of Chapter Three. Campbell moves metonymically from a mention of her mother's books—by "Shakespeare, Dickens, Sir Walter Scott and Longfellow"—to a description of the "Roman Empire" game, which involved playacting Caesar, Mark Anthony and Cleopatra (14). Campbell's disruption of chronology foregrounds the influence of European authors on

the children, thus making a deliberate point of cultural syncreticity. By emphasizing commonality instead of difference, Campbell destabilizes white readers' preconceptions about the Native Other. ⟨. . .⟩ At the same time as she defies their expectations, Campbell encourages white readers to enter the text through the door of familiarity rather than to look at the "Indian" through a "study window" ⟨Peggy Brizinski, *Knots in a String*, 1989, 300⟩. Disarmed, the reader is less likely to fetishize the information that soon follows about Native ways, such as:

> they would take us on long walks and teach us how to use the different herbs, roots and barks. We were taught to weave baskets from the red willow, and while we did these things together we were told the stories of our people. . . . My Cheechum believed with heart and soul in the little people. (18)

Campbell does not fetishize tradition and certainly does not long for a return to mystical, pre-colonial purity: the Metis are a product of the meeting of two cultures ⟨. . . .⟩ Bataille and Sands assert that the purpose of "Indian women who consciously" choose "to write their own life stories" is "to correct misinformation about Indians as savages and to bring the Indian and white worlds closer together" ⟨*American Indian Women, Telling Their Lives*, 1984, 21⟩. This assertion is supported by Campbell's statement at the end of *Halfbreed* that "I believe that one day, very soon, people will set aside their differences and come together as one. Maybe not because we love one another, but because we will need each other to survive" (184). In terms of literary hybridization, Bataille and Sands assert that *Halfbreed* "serves as further proof that the two modes of autobiography, written and oral, continue to exist simultaneously" (116). Indeed, Campbell's colloquial, conversational tone in the book—"I should tell you about our home now before I go any further" (16)—coupled with her use of (often humourous) anecdote and development by association rather than chronological sequence all represent traces of the oral tradition within the written form. Thus, Campbell's text is a site of cultural syncretism.
  —Jodi Lungren, "'Being a Half-breed': Discourses of Race and Cultural Syncreticity in the Works of Three Métis Women Writers," *Canadian Literature* 144 (Spring 1995): 72–74

BIBLIOGRAPHY

Halfbreed. 1973.
People of the Buffalo. 1976.
Little Badger and the Fire Spirit. 1977.
The Red Dress. 1977.
Riel's People. 1977.
Jessica (stage adaptation of *Halfbreed*, with Linda Griffiths). 1982.
The Book of Jessica: A Theatrical Transformation (with Linda Griffiths). 1989.

LOUISE ERDRICH

B. 1954

LOUISE ERDRICH was born in North Dakota in 1954, the daughter of a Turtle Mountain Chippewa mother and a father of German descent. She was educated at Dartmouth College, where she was a member of the first coeducational class and where she met her future husband, Michael Dorris; the two of them were at Dartmouth through the Native American program. Erdrich received her bachelor's degree in 1976 and went on to earn her M.F.A. in creative writing at The Johns Hopkins University. Erdrich and Dorris married in 1981 and began a career of intense collaboration, creating works whose every word, the authors have said, must be agreed upon between them. Before his death in 1997, the couple had three children together, in addition to three previously adopted by Dorris as a single parent.

Erdrich says she began writing as a poet, and she has published a volume of her collected poetry, *Jacklight* (1984). She began writing fiction because she wanted more room to tell a story. Storytelling, in her mind, is closely linked with the oral tradition of passing on history and cultural memories through fables and folklore.

Erdrich's first novel, *Love Medicine*, was published in 1984 and was named the best work of fiction by the National Book Critics Circle. The novel began a quartet that includes *The Beet Queen* (1986), *Tracks* (1988), and *The Bingo Palace* (1994), which together chronicle three generations of Native American and European immigrant families through interlocking stories told by different narrators. Many of these narratives reflect the oral quality of traditional storytelling that had earlier interested Erdrich: Nanapush in *Tracks*, for instance, in recounting a history to his granddaughter Lulu, creates the sense that we as readers are overhearing an old man tell a story. Erdrich uses the same characters in these novels, although a character who is central in one novel may be a supporting voice in another. The interlocking family stories were not published sequentially; *Tracks* was published third, although it functions as a "prequel" to the other novels, being set in the early part of the 20th century, just after the passage of the Dawes Act. Most of the material in *Love Medicine* and *The Beet Queen* is contemporary, as is that in *The Bingo Palace*. Together, the works create an entire history for the Chippewa (Anishinabe) tribe to which Erdrich belongs.

Erdrich's most recent novel, *Tales of Burning Love* (1996), returns to familiar terrain established in the quartet. Although it does not strictly continue the family stories and its events take place largely off the reservation and in Fargo, several of the quartet characters have cameo roles, creating a sense of continuity and further deepening readers' vision of the fictional world Erdrich has created.

CRITICAL EXTRACTS

LISSA SCHNEIDER

Louise Erdrich's *Love Medicine* has been regarded as simply a collection of short stories, lacking in novelistic unity and overriding structure. Yet despite shifts in narrative style and a virtual cacophony of often individually unreliable narrative voices, Erdrich successfully weds structure and theme, style and content. For the novel is as much about the act of storytelling as it is about the individual narratives and the symbols and interrelationships which weave them together thematically. In *Love Medicine*, storytelling constitutes both theme and style. Erdrich repeatedly shows how storytelling—characters sharing their troubles or their "stories" with one another—becomes a spiritual act, a means of achieving transformation, transcendence, forgiveness. And in this often comic novel, forgiveness is the true "love medicine," bringing a sense of wholeness, despite circumstances of loss or broken connections, to those who reach for it. Moreover, the novel is in itself the stylistic embodiment of Erdrich's theme; as a series of narratives or chapters/stories shared with the reader, the work as a whole becomes a kind of "love medicine" of forgiveness and healing in its own right.

The storytelling in the novel thus functions on manifold levels. With revealing insight, Kathleen Sands ⟨in *Studies in American Indian Literatures* 9, 1985⟩ has attributed the source of Erdrich's technique to "the secular anecdotal narrative process of community gossip" (14), and confirms that "ultimately it is a novel" (12), one that is "concerned as much with exploring the process of storytelling as with the story itself" (13). Sands, however, goes on to say that Erdrich's characters are unable "to give words to each other, except in rage or superficial dialogues that mask discomfort" (20), and focuses on the reader as the one who must "integrate the story into a coherent whole." She also suggests that such a reader must be "not some community member," but an "outsider" (15). This leads her to conclude that the novel "may not have the obvious spiritual power so often found in Indian fiction" (23), and in some respects underscores Nora Barry and Mary Prescott's critical assessment ⟨in *Critique* 30, 1989⟩ that "even sympathetic reviewers" tend to see Erdrich's characters as "doomed Chippewas" (123). In a more extreme vein, Louise Flavin ⟨in *Critique* 31, 1989⟩ submits that the novel's "diverse points of view" accentuate the "theme of the breakdown of relationships" and that it "suggests not tribal or family unity but separation and difference" (56), while Marvin Magalaner ⟨in *American Women Writing Fiction*, 1989⟩ points to themes of "entrapment and enclosure" (105) and curiously describes the characters as "savages now forced into tameness by material progress . . ." (104). By contrast, Barry and Prescott, in a sentiment closely echoed by Elizabeth Hanson, feel that *Love Medicine* "really celebrates Native American survival and credits spiritual values with that survival" (123). They attribute this survival to "a character's ability to internalize both the masculine and the feminine, the past and the present" (124).

I suggest that the means by which Erdrich's characters learn to internalize and integrate past with present is through the transformative power of story-telling. A non-Native reader, or any reader, is not the sole audience to these stories, for it is the characters themselves who, within the course of the narratives, begin this recovery of stories as they move beyond gossip to share with one another intimate revelations of highly personal desires, guilts, and troubles. It is in the personal stories that the characters *tell each other* that the real spiritual force of the novel can be felt.

Stories as "love medicine," moreover, provide the alternative in the novel to the characters' struggles with experiences of alcohol abuse, religious fanaticism, or compulsive sex relations, as well as the spiritual havoc that these kinds of seductive but hollow "love medicines" wreak on human relations. But although Erdrich focuses on the Chippewa experience, the troubles her characters experience are not exclusively "Indian problems." ⟨. . .⟩ These are problems common to every society, and the solution she posits is relevant for both Native and non-Native cultures alike. Forgiveness in *Love Medicine* is thus of the everyday variety, that which is extended from a child to a parent, a wife to a husband, brother to brother. Moreover, for Erdrich, forgiveness is not explanation, not unconditional, not forgetting. It is the transformation that comes through the sharing and recovery of stories, and the giving up of the notion of oneself as victim.

—Lissa Schneider, "*Love Medicine*: A Metaphor for Forgiveness," *Studies in American Indian Literatures* 4, no. 1 (Spring 1992): 1–2

ANNETTE VAN DYKE

Michael Dorris notes that the inspiration of the symbols of water and the water god shown in *Love Medicine* (and in *Tracks*) is one factor that distinguishes contemporary Chippewa from other rural North Dakota people ⟨Laura Coltelli, "Winged Words," 1990, 45⟩. ⟨. . .⟩

In Chippewa lore, the water spirits, who are also connected to fish, serpents or water-going snakes, water tigers, and lions, have a mixed reputation. They give power to control the waters and to net fish, but they are also seen as enemies to the prized bird spirits or Thunderbirds 〈. . . .〉 Connected to the danger of drowning and drawing storms over the water, they were given offerings of tobacco for safe passage 〈Norval Morriseau, *The Legends of My People*, 1965, 33〉.

The idea of being mated to the water man, and the conflicting powers of the Thunderbirds and water spirits, appear in a story collected by Henry Schoolcraft and published in 1856. In this story, entitled, "Wa-wa-be-zo-win," a jealous mother-in-law tricks her daughter-in-law into falling far out into Lake Superior. "After the wife had plunged into the lake, she found herself taken hold of by a water-tiger, whose tail twisted itself around her body, and drew her to the bottom. There she found a fine lodge, and all things ready for her reception, and she became the wife of the water-tiger" (194). After going to the lake the husband "painted his face black, and placed his spear upside down in the earth, and requested the Great Spirit to send lightning, thunder, and rain, in the hope that the body of his wife might arise from the water" (194).

In "The Underwater Lion," published by Victor Barnouw, two Chippewa women paddle their canoe across a large lake instead of around the edges, drawing the attention of "a bad manido":

> As they got to the middle, they crossed mud, and in the center was a hole of clear water. The water was swirling around the hole, and as they started to cross it, a lion came out of the middle and switched his tail across the boat, trying to turn it over. The girl picked up her little paddle and hit the lion's tail with it, saying, "Thunder is striking you." The paddle cut off the lion's tail, and the end dropped into the boat. When they picked it up, it was a solid piece of copper about two inches thick. . . . When they got across, the girl gave the piece of copper to her father, and he got rich through having it. The copper had certain powers. People would give her father a blanket just for a tiny piece of that copper. They would take that bit for luck in hunting and fishing, and some just kept it in their homes to bring good luck. (132–33)

Besides showing how thunder is called upon to defeat the water spirit, this story also illustrates the connection of the water spirit with copper. Both copper and white metal or hard white substance (mica) figure in the depiction of the water man in *Tracks*. In the Schoolcraft story, the tiger's tail becomes a belt made of "white metal" worn around the wife's waist.

Barnouw also comments that other stories associate the underwater horned serpent with an "erotic role . . . as a lover of girls" (137). In *Tracks*, Pauline describes the water spirit:

> Our mothers warn us that we'll think he's handsome, for he appears
> with green eyes, copper skin, a mouth tender as a child's. But if you
> fall into his arms, he sprouts horns, fangs, claws, fins. His feet are
> joined as one and his skin, brass scales, rings to the touch. You're fas-
> cinated, cannot move. He casts a shell necklace at your feet, weeps
> gleaming chips that harden into mica on your breasts. He holds you
> under. Then he takes the body of a lion, a fat brown worm, or a
> familiar man. He's made of gold. He's made of beach moss. He's a
> thing of dry foam, a thing of death by drowning, the death a
> Chippewa cannot survive. ⟨11⟩

Erdrich's portrayal of the water man combines many elements of the old stories—copper, a gleaming hard white substance, the erotic—as well as an
antagonism between thunder and the water spirit.

> —Annette Van Dyke, "Questions of the Spirit: Bloodlines in Louise Erdrich's Chippewa
> Landscape," *Studies in American Indian Literatures* 4, no. 1 (Spring 1992): 15–17

DANIEL CORNELL

In her 1988 novel, *Tracks*, Erdrich presents the history that precedes *Love
Medicine*. Through two narratives that alternate in time and point of view,
Erdrich recounts the displacement from native lands, the extensive kinship
networks, and the internecine struggles of the Chippewa people. One account
is given by Nanapush, who represents himself as a clever leader of the tribe,
situated between his Chippewa traditions and the U.S. government exploitation of American Indian peoples. At one point he says: "I had a Jesuit education in the halls of Saint John before I ran back to the woods and forgot all my
prayers" (*Tracks* 33). The other narrative is given by Pauline, a mixed breed
whose convent aspirations are realized at the novel's conclusion when she
becomes the Sister Leopolda of *Love Medicine*.

As a reader who had already encountered Pauline as Sister Leopolda in
Love Medicine, I was ready to read *Tracks* for the insight it would shed on her dis-
turbed psychology. And in fact, such an interpretation is easy to find. She concludes her narratives in *Tracks* with the explanation that she has been telling
her version of the events in order to explain why her soul is purified and ready
to receive convent vows ⟨. . . .⟩ Conflating American Indian and Judeo-
Christian religious traditions, Pauline sees herself as a visionary savior, the car-
rier of an understanding not available to those who have accepted the
blindness and deafness of a literal experience cut off from the symbolic. In her
mind, Misshepeshu, the Chippewa spirit of Lake Matchimanito, is identical to
the Christian devil, who is to be chained and thrown into the lake of fire. The
temptation for the reader is to understand Pauline's construction of her activ-

ity on the lake as evidence of insanity, to understand it as another example, like her refusal to experience the "pleasure" of feces or urine elimination more than once a day, as a misguided syncretism of American Indian and Christian religious traditions.

Additionally, the reader attempting to construct a single, unified point of view must ask how it is possible for Pauline to be narrating these events from her position of final mental disintegration at the novel's conclusion when she appears sane in the earlier parts of her narrative. In Nanapush, Erdrich presents the reader with a point of view that appears to contrast with Pauline's by its very stability. His narrative becomes the interpretive grid against which the reader evaluates Pauline, and in his judgment she is not trustworthy 〈. . . .〉 According to Nanapush, the reader who accepts Pauline's account is merely a lover of dirt. Thus Erdrich implicates her readers in an objectification of Pauline if they accept Nanapush's point of view as the literal ground from which to reconstruct Pauline's narrative.

However, there is another interpretation of the character of Pauline if the power relations in the novel are examined. These power relations point to the close relation between racism and sexism that according to Trinh T. Minh-ha is authorized by imposing a dominant Euroamerican point of view:

> The pitting of anti-racist and anti-sexist struggles against one another allows some vocal fighters to dismiss blatantly the existence of either racism or sexism within their lines of action, as if oppression only comes in separate, monolithic form. Thus, to understand how pervasively dominance operates via the concept of hegemony or of absent totality in plurality is to understand that the work of decolonization will have to continue within the women's movements. 〈*Woman, Native, Other,* 1989, 104〉

If the power relations between Nanapush and Pauline are examined in light of gender, Pauline becomes more than the neurotic wallflower Nanapush represents her as, embraiding lies to compensate for her lack of sexual appeal. Rather, she takes up a position that in a male authored order belongs solely to men: she demands the equality of a constituting gaze, the privilege of being a constitutive subject. It is not lies that she constructs but her own right to look. In the process she reveals the sexual politics within Nanapush's narrative discourse.

—Daniel Cornell, "Woman Looking: Revis(ion)ing Pauline's Subject Position in Louise Erdrich's *Tracks,*" *Studies in American Indian Literatures* 4, no. 1 (Spring 1992): 50–52

SUSAN STANFORD FRIEDMAN

In a scathing review ("Here's an Odd Artifact for the Fairy-Tale Shelf," 1986), Leslie Marmon Silko condemns Louise Erdrich's *The Beet Queen* (1986) to the "same shelf that holds the *Collected Thoughts of Edwin Meese on First Amendment Rights* and Grimm's *Fairy Tales*" (184). Silko finds the prose of the second novel in Erdrich's projected tetralogy set in the reservation and off-reservation environs of Argus, North Dakota, to be "dazzling and sleek," a "'poet's prose'" that marks the novel as "an outgrowth of academic, post-modern, so-called experimental influences" (178–79). Silko reads the novel as a betrayal of Indian history and realities, as a postmodern erasure of the political forces that shape Indian life. Erdrich's North Dakota, she writes, "is an oddly rarified place in which the individual's own psyche, not racism or poverty, accounts for all conflict and tension" (180).

In what sense is Erdrich's work "political," if not "polemical"? Where does *Tracks*—drafted well before she published *Love Medicine* (1984) and *The Beet Queen* (1986), but not published until 1988—fit into debates about representing the political and the postmodern in the contemporary novel? In spite of the novel's equally dazzling poet's prose, Silko might regard more positively the novel's open reference to the starvation, disease, and loss among the Chippewa that resulted from contact with Euro-American culture and the land allotment policies of the United States government in the late nineteenth and early twentieth centuries. But I do not believe that Erdrich's representation of the political in *Tracks* resides in any greater or lesser narrative inscription of historical "fact." Rather, the political vision of the novel emerges out of its complex, often hilarious, and ultimately indeterminate play with questions of identity and spirituality as these are constituted in culture and history. Erdrich's desire to avoid the polemical, I want to suggest, resides in her distrust of a fundamentalist certainty about fixed truth and her embrace of a syncretist politics based in fluid, multi-faceted, shape-changing, hard-won truths.

Highlighting the importance of spirituality in many Native American cultures and literatures, *Tracks* can be read as a religious parable open to two seemingly contradictory readings: first, as a promotion of Anishinabe spirituality; and second, as an exploration of religious syncretism. On the one hand, as an expression of identity politics, the novel overtly sets up a contrast between Nanapush as the reliable narrator who retains his Anishinabe religion and the unreliable narrator, the convert Pauline whose self-hatred takes the form of a denial of her Indian heritage and the adoption of a self-destructive Catholicism. But on the other hand, as an expression of religious syncretism, the novel covertly uses Nanapush and Pauline to draw significant parallels between Anishinabe spirituality and Catholic mysticism. From this perspective, the novel acknowledges an interpenetration and hybridization of Anishinabe and European spirituality and identity.

    —Susan Stanford Friedman, "Identity Politics, Syncretism, Catholicism, and Anishinabe Religion in Louise Erdrich's *Tracks*," *Religion & Literature* 26, no. 1 (Spring 1994): 107–8

NANCY J. PETERSON

Erdrich's novel *Tracks*, published in 1988, almost seems to answer Silko's criticisms of *The Beet Queen* by overtly engaging political and historical issues. But writing such a novel did not come easily to Erdrich: she put the original 400-page manuscript for *Tracks* aside for ten years, and only after she had worked backward in time from *Love Medicine* to *The Beet Queen* did she take it up again and begin to link it to her already completed novels about contemporary generations of Chippewa and immigrant settlers in North Dakota.

Erdrich's difficulty in fleshing out this historical saga is symptomatic of a crisis: the impossibility of writing traditional history in a postmodern, postrepresentational era. ⟨. . .⟩

Since traditional written history, based on documents, is another kind of violence inflicted on oppressed peoples, *Tracks* features oral history. The opening of the novel uses oral storytelling markers: the narrator does not name himself, as he would not in a traditional face-to-face storytelling situation, nor is the addressee named except to designate her relationship to the narrator ("Granddaughter"); the last two paragraphs ⟨of the opening five⟩ contain a rhetorical pattern typically associated with orality, repetition with variations ("I guided," "I saw," "I trapped"). Other oral markers signify Erdrich's rejection of the language of documents: Nanapush refers to "the spotted sickness," not to smallpox or measles; he uses traditional oral tribal names (Nadouissioux, Anishinabe) rather than anglicized textual ones (Sioux, Chippewa); he speaks of "a storm of government papers" instead of naming specific documents affecting the tribe. The turn to oral history in *Tracks* signals the need for indigenous peoples to tell their own stories and their own histories.

But the evocation of the oral in a written text implicates this counterhistory in the historical narrative that it seeks to displace. *Tracks* renders a history of Anishinabe dispossession that moves within and against an academic account of this history. Indeed, the need to know history as it is constructed both orally and textually is indicated by the contextual phrases that begin each chapter: first a date, including the designation of season(s) and year(s), then a phrase in Anishinabe followed by an English translation. This information establishes two competing and contradictory frames of reference: one associated with orality, a seasonal or cyclic approach to history, a precontact culture; the other linked with textuality, a linear or progressive approach to history, a postcontact culture. Erdrich creates a history of dispossession that moves between these frames, that is enmeshed in the academic narrative of dates and of causes and effects concerning the loss of land.

—Nancy J. Peterson, "History, Postmodernism, and Louise Erdrich's *Tracks*," *Publications of the Modern Language Association* 109, no. 5 (October 1994): 982, 985–86

DENNIS M. WALSH AND ANN BRALEY

Ojibway (Chippewa/Anishnabeg) myth and ceremony in relation to Louise Erdrich's fiction has been the subject of seminal literary study of her works. James McKenzie's tracking of "the traditional Chippewa trickster hero and powerful spirit, Nanabozho," or Nanapush, in Erdrich's *Love Medicine* was written in evident distress at the lack of comprehension by early reviewers. McKenzie concludes,

> The pattern of the novel's development in the June-Gerry-Lipsha stories suggests not only the survival but also a renewal of Chippewa culture "in the wake of the catastrophe," as Erdrich so aptly describes the case . . . . The novel knows and celebrates the human wealth of each of its separate characters as well as the collective wealth of the Chippewa nation, a culture still present in the face of several centuries of murderous opposition. ⟨"Lipsha's Good Road Home," 1986, 63⟩

Ann Braley has documented Ojibway myth and ceremony in *Love Medicine* (1984), Ojibway Mother Earth characters, a Weendigo (the insatiable one), Odaemin (the culture's first medicine man), Geezhig (a voyager to the Land of the Dead), Sky Woman, widespread water imagery reflecting Ojibway myth, and turtle and deer myth ⟨master's thesis, Idaho State University, 1993⟩. Moreover, McKenzie and Lydia Schultz have written about Erdrich's use of oral storytelling in *Love Medicine* ⟨"Fragments and Ojibwa Stories," 1991⟩.

Erdrich's *Tracks* (1988) allows open season for those hunting Indian elements. Perhaps the fullest treatment is that of Jennifer Sergi, who finds that "(1) [Erdrich] captures the form and purpose of oral storytelling; (2) she includes the contents of Chippewa myth and legend; (3) and she preserves these cultural traditions in a voice that harks back to the old as it creates anew." Besides the Nanapush storyteller, we find "windigos, manitous, burying the dead in trees, dreamcatchers, a Jeesewinini (medicine man), and 'Anishinabe characters, the old gods,' as Nanapush refers to them" ⟨"Storytelling," 1990⟩.

In *The Beet Queen* (1986), because white, Euro-American characters appear to dominate the novel, the connections to Ojibway culture are not as clear as those in *Love Medicine* and *Tracks*. However, Susan Perez Castillo contends that, in *The Beet Queen* "we encounter the Reservation more as absence than presence, more as latency than as statement, in contrast to the arid reality of the small town of Argus, North Dakota" ⟨"Post-modernism, Native American Literature and the Real," 1991, 286⟩. By taking us off the reservation, perhaps Erdrich intends not to show what is present in Argus but what is missing. In *Love Medicine*, Erdrich shows contemporary Ojibway people surviving in and around a dominant white culture. In *Tracks*, she shows the Ojibway's initial loss of land and culture to an increasingly present white culture and the Indians' subsequent struggle to hold on to tradition. But *The Beet Queen*, a darkly comic, ironic, and sometimes fantastic depiction of the off-reservation town of Argus, shows the dominant culture in a way that reflects Ojibway worldview, which is "impossibly everywhere and nowhere all at once" (p. 41). Erdrich achieves this depiction in several ways: through humor, through an exploration of the significance of "land" and kinship/community, and through Indian characters.

    —Dennis M. Walsh and Ann Braley, "The Indianness of Louise Erdrich's *The Beet Queen*: Latency as Presence," *American Indian Culture and Research Journal* 18, no. 3 (1994): 1–2

BARBARA L. PITTMAN

Erdrich uses the road motif for the architectonic functions of opening and closing her novel ⟨*Love Medicine*⟩, as well as for representing chance encounters between characters. *Love Medicine* opens with June Kashpaw "walking down the clogged main street of oil boomtown Williston, North Dakota," waiting for the bus that is to take her home along another road. She is "killing time" (*LM*, 1) until a chance encounter finds her driving "down the street in . . . [a] Silverado pickup" with a "mud engineer" named "Andy" (*LM*, 3). Finally, "far out of town on a county road" (*LM*, 4), they attempt to have sex, and June decides to walk home, going "*off the road*" (*LM*, 6; emphasis added) and through the fields, despite a winter storm, a storm in which she finally dies.

The closing episode has June's son Lipsha Morrissey driving the highways toward home after having helped his father, Gerry Nanapush, escape to Canada. He comes to "the bridge over the boundary river," where he stops to remember such things as an old ceremony of offering "tobacco to the water," his mother, and "sunken cars" (*LM*, 271). After recalling the myth of the river once having been "an ancient ocean," Lipsha faces the "truth" of the "dry land" and continues on the "good road" home (*LM*, 272).

In between these two homeward-bound events are at least five other major encounters and dozens of smaller, sometimes trivial, references to roads. Most of the major encounters are moments of crisis expressed through sex or death and consequently contributing to both the establishment and the dissolution of the central family groups. The accumulated road references reinforce the concrete representation of time and space, and, because of the probability of chance encounters in such places, also reinforce the absurd nature of man's existence in time and space. The motif of the road as a way of representing time and space in the novel has a particular significance in relationship to the picaresque.

Because the chronotope of the road is most familiar in the Euro-American tradition through the picaresque, any subsequent use of this chronotope, while re-accentuated, retains a "'stylistic aura'" from "that genre in which the given word usually functions. It is an echo of the generic whole that resounds in the word" ⟨M. M. Bakhtin, *Speech Genres and Other Late Essays*, 1986, 87–88⟩. This generic echo, resounding here in the chronotopic motif, recalls typical picaresque motifs and prompts the reader to translate them into this text. In the picaresque novel, a long winding road determines the plot, as it "passes through *familiar territory*, and not through some exotic *alien world*"; it reveals "the *sociohistorical heterogeneity* of one's own country" in the variety of events that take place along it ⟨Bakhtin, *The Dialogic Imagination*, 245⟩. The first effect of reading *Love Medicine* through the picaresque lens is to recognize in its disconnected road scenes, which involve a number of the novel's main characters, a movement away from linear continuity toward a postmodern, antilinear discontinuity—a formal depiction closer to the picaresque condition of "continuous dis-integration." As metaphor, the discontinuous road seems to comment on the breakup of the Native American tribal community as it tries to exist both within and without the dominant culture of Euro-America. Erdrich depicts pieces or fragments of roads separated by postmodern silence and narrated by isolated voices; the events that occur on them share the characters' sense of fragmentation and isolation.

There are several other implications and advantages of reading *Love Medicine* as a version of the picaresque. Because the spatial aspect of the novel (seen in the road) is more developed than the temporal, the year designations at the beginning of each chapter can be read as Erdrich's imposition of a definite, if mechanical, temporal structure to achieve a balance between time and space. The traditional picaresque depicts a socially diverse world through a dual focus on adventure and the development of the hero as he interacts with such a world. Erdrich's episodic, multi-narrative style duplicates or improves upon the picaresque by setting a diverse group of protagonists in a diverse world. Just as the early picaresque was "a reaction against Renaissance humanism, in its more classicizing and idealizing modes" ⟨Walter L. Reed, *An Exemplary History of the Novel*, 1981, 30⟩, *Love Medicine* is a satire on the romanticization of Indians, not only in its honest depiction of alcoholism and physical abuse but also in such scenes as those in which Nector poses for the *"Plunge of the Brave"* (*LM*, 91)—a painting that shows the Western ideal of the naked, noble savage—or works in movies, always as a dying brave. Nector is used again for a picaresque as well as postmodern engagement with the canon "through a critical lampooning of some of [society's] favorite literature" ⟨Barbara A. Babcock, in *The Reversible World*, 1978, 100⟩—specifically *Moby-Dick*. By having Nector live the "marginal man's career of deception" ⟨Reed, 71⟩ through his identification with both Ishmael and Ahab, Erdrich engages in a dialogue with the canon that subverts its power and calls attention to barriers between oral and written traditions. When Nector tells his mother, Rushes Bear, that the novel is about a "great white whale," she wants to know what "they got to wail about, those whites" (*LM*, 91).

Although Euro-American–trained readers may initially read *Love Medicine* as inscribed with the picaresque, by positioning themselves as outsiders they can create an atmosphere in which alternative meanings are sought and welcomed. When such readers then seek out Native American literary traditions and attempt to reconcile them with their own, they may discover that narratives "do make things happen" ⟨Arnold Krupat, "The Dialogic of Silko's *Storyteller*, 1989, 63⟩.

> —Barbara L. Pittman, "Cross-cultural Reading and Generic Transformations: The Chronotope of the Road in Erdrich's *Love Medicine*," *American Literature* 67, no. 4 (December 1995): 779–81

JOHN PURDY

One of the attractive characteristics of *Love Medicine* is its subtle complexity; it offers a diversity of perceptions through a multilayered narrative in which each character's story is centered in a relatively small, seemingly loose-knit community of characters and events. Much like the novels of modernists such as Woolf or Faulkner (who was one influence upon Erdrich's art and to whom she is most often compared), hers evolves through each successive telling of events, and builds toward understanding by requiring the reader to adopt a participatory role and thereby invest in the lives and events it portrays. This process is enhanced by Erdrich's use of first-person narratives that engage us directly in the discourse. We are spoken to, sometimes like amateur ethnographers and at others like familiar confidants; we are asked to respond; we are required to build connections and patterns; and we are satisfied when our efforts in making the story work out are rewarded. Unlike Faulkner or Woolf, however, Erdrich describes "life on the rez," the funnel end of colonialism in the United States of America, and it is to her credit that she entices non-Native American readers into a network of history and a present largely foreign to them, and she does so in compelling ways. ⟨. . .⟩

⟨. . . It⟩ is June who is the heart of the novel, a referential "center" for all the other characters, and it is she to whom we are first introduced. Her section of the first chapter is told in the third person and in past tense, which in effect removes her own "voice" (and vision) from the novel. It is also very brief, yet it effectively smooths the ground for all that is to follow and for all that is to become significant. In fact, one means of highlighting the accomplishments of the novel is to read these few opening pages immediately after finishing the last. For instance, the closing line of the novel—"So there was nothing to do but cross the water, and bring her home"—takes on added dimension from the ideas and images presented in June's section, for she is as much the antecedent to the pronoun "her" as the car Lipsha is driving over the bridge on his return home, to the reservation.

The first pages seem to describe a bleak, rootless, unsatisfying life. In fact, they conform to, but engage dramatically, the long-held stereotypes of American Indians found in popular literature written by non-Native writers from Purchas to Thoreau to Kesey. More specifically, Erdrich directly confronts those stereotypes of Native women as "loose" drunks whose ill fates are foregone conclusions. In fact, one early newspaper reviewer clearly demonstrates how pervasive these images have become; for her, June is simply "a drunken prostitute," worthy of mention it seems, but not of understanding, or contextualizing. Thus the popular media perform. To Erdrich's credit, she does not avoid the fundamental issues behind such easy generalizations, nor the materialistic bias upon which racist stereotypes are based. Instead, she opens her first novel with this all-too-familiar image of poverty, yet does not allow readers to wallow in the comfort of moralistic judgments from a distance: we cannot dismiss with easy categorization. June, we learn, is simply looking for love, as she has all her life, to heal the hurt and loss suffered when her mother dies, leaving her child alone in the "bush" to fend for herself. June survives, and from this experience comes pain, but also a strength. In the opening pages, near the end of her life, she is not the helpless pawn of fate, or of poverty, or of men as much as she is, somehow, a proud, deliberate force who initiates and directs the actions described. In effect, Erdrich devotes the remainder of the text to shaking the assumptions upon which ethnocentric pronouncements— based upon false information and emerging through privilege—are made. This is no small task.

Like many other contemporary Native novels, *Love Medicine* begins with a homecoming, what Bill Bevis has termed a "Homing In." However, unlike Archilde in D'Arcy McNickle's *The Surrounded*, or Abel in N. Scott Momaday's *House Made of Dawn*, June's return is subtly veiled, for she does not return "physically." Instead, she comes home as vivid, warm, unshakable memories for all the characters who speak to us after, or more pointedly, she comes home as a character in the stories they tell, the oral literary canon they all share that tells them who they are in relation to others. She dies; at least, we are told that she is brought home and buried, although like Albertine—June's "niece" who is away at school and whose own homecoming provides us with the initial first-person narrative—we do not "witness" the act: it is not made an event in the novel. Although it may seem inconsequential, this is a significant point for it establishes June as a disembodied, silent, yet palpable presence—a nebulous yet powerful center—throughout the stories and lives of other characters. Furthermore, it draws attention to the details of the brief description of June's final moments, where Erdrich presents not June's death, but her transcendence (for lack of a better term). This, of course, should undermine the reader's ability to consider her death a justifiable punishment for a "freewheeling" lifestyle. Life and death, particularly on reservations, are not that simple.

—John Purdy, "Building Bridges: Crossing the Waters to a *Love Medicine* (Louise Erdrich)," in *Teaching American Ethnic Literatures: Nineteen Essays*, ed. John R. Maitino and David R. Peck (Albuquerque: University of New Mexico Press, 1996), 83–85

B I B L I O G R A P H Y

Imagination. 1981.

Jacklight. 1984.

Love Medicine. 1984.

The Beet Queen. 1986.

Tracks. 1988.

Baptism of Desire. 1989.

The Crown of Columbus (with Michael Dorris). 1991.

Route Two (with Michael Dorris). 1991.

The Bingo Palace. 1994.

The Blue Jay's Dance: A Birth Year. 1995.

Grandmother's Pigeon. 1996.

Tales of Burning Love. 1996.

JOY HARJO

B. 1951

JOY HARJO was born in Tulsa, Oklahoma, in 1951 and is a member of the Creek (Muskogee) tribe. She lived in Oklahoma until she was 14, when she moved to Albuquerque. She received her B.A. from the University of New Mexico and went on to earn an M.F.A. from the Iowa Writer's Workshop. Known primarily as a poet, Harjo has also studied painting and worked as a screenwriter, and she occasionally plays in a jazz band.

Harjo draws on all her interests—art, music, history, politics—to create her poems, often combining languages and images from seemingly disparate realms. Although she is not a Navajo, for instance, she sometimes uses that language because she likes its singsong, chantlike quality. Her poetry draws quite strongly on traditional Native American themes and motifs, but Harjo points out that her experiences have been predominantly urban; unlike many of her contemporaries, she is not a "reservation Indian." She says that she deliberately plays with people's expectations of what it means to be an Indian by manipulating stereotypes and settings in her poems. So, for instance, in her poem "Origin," one of the characters finds release through high-speed interstate driving, rather than through an ancient Indian ritual. Harjo frequently juxtaposes past and present, urban and rural, into poetry that reminds us of the importance of memory—that it is memory that gives us a home.

Another task for Harjo's poetry, she says, is to put to rest the idea that she, or any Native American woman writer, represents an entire culture. It is the individual experience that matters, she says, and her experience is different from that of a woman raised in the Laguna tribe or the Cree, or even from that of another Muscogee raised in a different part of the country. Harjo takes pleasure in such differences, even as she asserts that one of her hopes for the future is that such categories of difference (like male/female, Indian/non-Indian) will cease to matter. The writers whom she counts as influences illustrate her belief in cross-cultural dialogue: Galway Kinnell, Adrienne Rich, Audre Lorde, Leslie Silko, and June Jordan. She also cites as important the music of John Coltrane and Billie Holiday and has dedicated poems to both artists.

CRITICAL EXTRACTS

LYNDA KOOLISH

In Joy Harjo's "Explosion," the imagined "violent birth of horses" becomes another kind of birth: the poet's explosion into language out of speechlessness ⟨in *She Had Some Horses*, 1983, 68–69⟩. Each has a wild, astonishing beauty to it, volcanic and galvanizing. The poet and the horses "bursting out of the crazy earth" are one, their unwillingness to be tamed, contained, hers. Their urgency, wisdom, and magic, hers as well. She sees the horses through an act of volition, a willingness to apprehend, to be alive to all that is. She knows that like the poem itself, and the vision of transformation, articulation, and power which it represents, the horses which she sees will be invisible to some. But she writes for those who, in reading her words, will be able to

> . . . see the horses with their hearts of sleeping volcanoes
> and . . . be rocked awake
> past their bodies
>
> to see who they have become.

In another poem from *She Had Some Horses*, Harjo accesses the power of language to make sense out of an often brutally senseless world. In "Rain," a young man loses his life in a truck accident. What remains—for the poet and for the reader—is not the violence of his death but rather the poet's healing and transfiguring vision of "a light in the river / folding open and open / blood, heart and stones / shimmering like the Milky Way" ⟨17⟩. Through language, the scene of Bobby's death is recreated and given its meaning by the poet, not by the outside world.

> —Lynda Koolish, "The Bones of This Body Say, Dance: Self-Empowerment in Contemporary Poetry by Women of Color," in *A Gift of Tongues: Critical Challenges in Contemporary American Poetry*, ed. Marie Harris and Kathleen Aguero (Athens, GA: University of Georgia Press, 1987), 45–46

PATRICIA CLARK SMITH AND PAULA GUNN ALLEN

Harjo turns to the theme of human erotic connections with spirit figures who embody the land in her many poems about the moon. In them, the moon appears not as symbol and certainly not as background lighting, but as a full, intelligent female person. That the moon should be so important in Harjo's work makes sense given her woman-centeredness and her representation of herself as a woman on the move. The womanness of the moon is in almost all cultures, and she can be there for the wanderer in Anchorage or Hong Kong; like Harjo, she is a traveler too. The moon, that medieval emblem of instability for Western Europeans, is a stable comforter for Harjo; in "Heartbeat," Noni Daylight drops acid and drives through Albuquerque with a pistol cradled in her lap. In the middle of this nighttown horror, "Noni takes the hand of the moon / that she knows is in control overhead." The poem concludes, "It is not the moon, or the pistol in her lap / but a fierce anger / that will free her." Even so, given that Noni has yet to find that anger, the moon is the only entity who remains steady, who reaches out to Noni in a time when "these nights, she wants out."

And yet the comforting moon Harjo knows is also as completely herself and as mysterious as ⟨Luci Tapahonso's⟩ Snake-man or ⟨Leslie Silko's⟩ mountain ka'tsinas. Harjo conveys this moon's wildness and independent life beautifully in "Moonlight": "I know when the sun is in China / because the night-shining other-light / crawls into my bed. She is moon." Harjo imagines the other side of the world,

> in Hong Kong, Where someone else has also
> awakened, the night thrown back and asked,
> "Where is the moon, my lover?"
> And from here I always answer in my dreaming,
> "The last time I saw her, she was in the arms
> of another sky."

What matters most about Harjo's moon is her ability as a living spirit to enter into the sort of dialogue with people that reassures them, no matter where they are, of their own lives and their connection with wilderness. In "September Moon," as Harjo and her children try to cross Albuquerque's Central Avenue in the midst of State Fair traffic, she encounters the moon rising out of the trapped air of the urban Rio Grande Valley:

> I was fearful of traffic
> trying to keep my steps and the moon was east,
> ballooning out of the mountain ridge, out of smokey clouds
> out of any skin that was covering her. Naked.
> Such beauty.
>   Look.
> We are alive. The woman of the moon looking
> at us, and we are looking at her, acknowledging
> each other.

The land and the person acknowledging each other as loving beings, sensate and sensual, their lives inextricably woven together in Spider Woman's web—this is what lies at the heart of American Indian ritual and southwestern American Indian women's writing.

> —Patricia Clark Smith and Paula Gunn Allen, "Earthy Relations, Carnal Knowledge," in *The Desert Is No Lady: Southwestern Landscapes in Women's Writing and Art*, ed. Vera Norwood and Janice Monk (New Haven: Yale University Press, 1987), 195–96

MARILYN KALLET

⟨Interview with Joy Harjo by Marilyn Kallet⟩

MK: *What were your beginnings as a writer?*

JH: I could look at this in a couple of ways. One is to look at the myths and stories of the people who formed me in the place where I entered the world. . . . Another way is to look at when I first consciously called myself a writer. I started writing poetry when I was pretty old, actually—I was about twenty-two. I committed to poetry the day I went in to my painting teacher who mentored me and expected a fine career in painting for me, and told him I was switching my major to poetry. I made the decision to learn what poetry could teach me. It was a painful choice. I come from a family of Muscogee painters. My grandmother and my great-aunt both got their B.F.A.'s in Art in the early 1900s. And from the time I was very small you could always find me drawing, whether it was in the dirt or on paper. That was one thing that made me happy. . . . I always said that when I grow up I am going to be a painter, I am going to be an artist. Then I made the decision to work with words and the power of words, to work with language, yet I approach the art as a visual artist. From childhood my perceptions were through the eye of a painter. I feel any writer serves many aspects of culture, including language, but you also serve history, you serve the mythic structure that you're part of, the people, the earth, and so on—and none of these are separate.

MK: *It seems like almost any question we ask about your writing, about your cultural background, is going to lead us in the same paths of discussion about your family life, your tribal life, and your life as a writer.*

JH: Well, they are not separate, really. Though the way I've come to things is very different from say, Beth Cuthand, who is a Cree writer from Saskatchewan, or Leslie Silko from Laguna. There's a tendency in this country to find one writer of a particular ethnicity and expect her to speak for everyone and expect her experience to be representative of all Native women and all Native people. My experience is very different from Silko's and Cuthand's, although it's similar in the sense of a generational thing, of certain influences on us and influences we have on each other. But my experience has been predominantly urban. I did not grow up on a reservation—we don't even have a reservation. There are more rural areas where the people are. I'm not a full-blood, and yet I am a full member of my (Muscogee) tribe, and I have been a full member of my tribe since my birth into the tribe. I find some people have preconceived ideas—I was talking to this guy on the plane and he says, "Well, you don't fit my idea of an Indian." What does that mean? I think for most people in this country, it means to be a Hollywood version of a Plains tribe, as falsely-imagined 100 or 150 years ago. Most people in this country have learned all they know about Indian people from movies and television. . . .

MK: *Certain books have helped to popularize Plains culture.* Black Elk Speaks *is taught most often at the university.* . . .

JH: And even then it's a perversion of what it means to be an Indian in this country—how do you translate context? Within my tribe you have people who are very grounded in the traditions, and are very close to the land. Then you have people who are heavily involved in church; some are involved in both; some live in Tulsa, which is where I grew up; others live all over but are still close to that place which is home. It is more than land—but of the land— a tradition of mythologies, of ongoing history . . . it forms us.
      —Marilyn Kallet, "In Love and War and Music: An Interview with Joy Harjo," *The Kenyon Review* 15, no. 3 (Summer 1993): 57–58

NANCY LANG

Within her varied urban landscapes, Harjo's poetry most clearly illustrates the multi-voiced nature of any marginalized poetry, and of Native American women's poetry in particular. On the one hand, after a first reading Harjo may seem to be writing out of the city-as-subject tradition of American poets like Walt Whitman, Carl Sandburg, Hart Crane, and William Carlos Williams. On the other hand, her city landscapes do not reflect promise and optimistic excitement, as do many urban settings of earlier white male American poets. Rather, Harjo's cities resonate with Native American memories of an endless and ongoing history of Eurocentric and genocidal social and political policies: war, forced removal, imposed education, racism, and assimilationism.

    While Allen, Hogan, and Rose often use the contemporary city as negative physical setting in a variety of ways, Harjo especially foregrounds the psychological and spiritual impacts, and the resulting personal chaos, of urban life on the Native American survivor. 〈. . .〉

It is with the poems of *She Had Some Horses* (1983), and especially with one of her most powerful poems, "The Woman Hanging From the Thirteenth Floor," that Harjo fully articulates the interlocked problems of unnamed fears and the resulting speechlessness of an oppressed and dispossessed woman. Told in the flat, seemingly unemotional voice of a dispassionate observer, this highly rhythmic prose poem tells the story of a young Native American mother caught in the trap of her life and trying to find some way, any way, out of her nightmare. Memories of her own traditionally-oriented childhood, her family, her children, and her lovers no longer sustain her, as "her mind chatters like neon and northside bars" (23). Hanging in space, thirteen floors up from the city streets of an East Chicago ghetto, she hears some people screaming that she should jump, while others try to help her with their prayers. At the end of the poem "she would speak" (23), but *will* she take charge of her own life? Or, is she doomed to death and oblivion?

In an interview with Laura Coltelli, Harjo tells the story of how "The Woman Hanging From the Thirteenth Floor" came to be written. Growing out of a private experience she had at the Chicago Indian Center, the poem reflects Harjo's invented persona and voice, yet people continue to come up to her at readings and say they know a woman like that; or they have read such a story in the newspaper, but the incident occurred somewhere else ⟨*Winged Words*, 1990, 62⟩. Whether by accident or by design, Harjo has constructed a folkloric, urban Native American example of every woman's ultimate fear, the fear of being totally and absolutely frozen and helpless, without the power to speak, unable to function, and therefore not able to choose either life or death for herself.

Harjo writes a deliberately incomplete ending to the unnamed woman's story, because the woman considers letting go and falling, as well as trying again by climbing back through her apartment window. In this way, Harjo gives her readers the freedom to become writers, since the unnamed woman's story has the potential to become every woman's multi-voiced yet muted struggle against fear, depression, death, and oblivion.

—Nancy Lang, "'Twin Gods Bending Over': Joy Harjo and Poetic Memory," *MELUS* 18, no. 3 (Fall 1993): 41–42, 44–45

JENNY GOODMAN

Harjo's "Crossing Water" ⟨. . . .⟩ is certainly not one of the most overtly "political" poems in *In Mad Love and War*, a book that includes poems like the frequently cited and anthologized poem of historical witness, "For Anna Mae Pictou Aquash, Whose Spirit Is Present Here and in the Dappled Stars (for we remember the story and must tell it again so we may all live)." However,

"Crossing Water" does directly address the constraints on a poet who seeks to redefine both politics and poetry. A half-page prose-like poem that appears in a single block, it begins,

> I return like a detective to the dance floor in New York, or was it someplace else invented to look like October? I turn back to a music the d.j. never played because the room was too blue for falling angels. Nothing by Aretha, nothing by chance. A woman chased by spirits kept asking you to dance, made a gift of her hands. I add her to the evidence: we were there. She was a witness but I don't have her name. Or yours or mine, or was the shift in axis an event in the imagination? (46)

In the midst of this lyrical account, the poet-speaker then breaks off, saying,

> I should be writing poems to change the world. They would appear as a sacrifice of deer for the starving. Or poems of difficulty to place my name in the Book of Poets. (46)

These words address "fellow poets," "teachers" and "critics," ⟨. . .⟩, the voices of whom are as much inside the poet-speaker's head as they are printed in literary journals or political magazines. But the poet proceeds to write neither an obviously political poem nor a modernist-influenced "poem of difficulty." She continues her dream-like account of an erotic encounter:

> Instead I walk back through the dark in my shoes the color of hearts to find us embraced in a ring of smoke. Hey, I wanted you in your jeans and casual sweater with your caramel lips. (46)

She calls into question our notions of accessibility versus difficulty, and our notions about what constitutes political content.

The poem seems accessible, from one standpoint, because the speaker seems to be the poet herself, recounting a shared memory to a lover. The diction could be construed as "simplified," ⟨. . .⟩ and there are references to American popular culture: a dance floor, a d.j., music by "Aretha." We even get a bald conversational statement, an expression of sexual desire we might associate with a radio song: "Hey, I wanted you in your jeans and casual / sweater with your caramel lips." Yet the manner in which this poem engages readers cannot be accounted for by the commonsense interpretations encouraged by easy, personal poems. We are not placed in the position of mere observers of the authentic experience of the poet, of an event that "really happened" to her. Some of the poem's language is deeply musical (music provides both themes and formal strategies in this poem): the description of the imagined dance club tells us "the room was too blue for falling angels." In addition, internal rhymes and assonance help to create the sensual, rhythmic, dream-like atmosphere of the poem: "Nothing by Aretha, / nothing by chance. A woman chased by spirits kept asking you to dance, / made a gift of her hands. I add her to the evidence." Finally, the subtle, jazz-like phrasing that ends the poem evokes the sense of a memory that hovers between material reality and dream: "The / evidence floats by like rings over sweet water. Like rings over sweet / water" (46).

The mixture of cultures that informs the poem's imagery and intellectual content makes additional demands upon readers, who must perform imaginative work to put the various associations together. Native American references appear in the statement "A woman chased by spirits kept asking you to dance" and in the simile of "a sacrifice of deer for the starving," which, as we have seen, expresses the poet's conception of poems for political change. The mention of "poems / of difficulty to place my name in the Book of the Poets" introduces a second register of discourse; it is surely an allusion to the aesthetics of the great modernists that an American poet learns. The popular music and imaginary "dance floor in New York" bring in yet a third register of language and experience.

The conversational diction and frank eroticism of the poem (without irony, without reference to a more spiritual eroticism of a mythic past) do not seem to fit in a modernist-influenced "poem of difficulty." In addition, unlike some experimental poems in what has become the modernist tradition, this poem does not demand a specialized education from its readers. Though certain references or juxtapositions might be unfamiliar to some readers, the poem does not set itself apart from the vocabulary of everyday experience, if that experience is coupled with some imagination. (I don't know the specific rite associated with the sacrifice of deer, for instance, but I understand that Harjo is talking about something sacred. I imagine, further, that the sacrifice affirms the group's responsibility to those who suffer and who die because of injustice.) Harjo's poetry does challenge dominant cultural *understandings* of our lives, however. It denies readers the easy, isolating, and, ultimately, impotent role of voyeurs, just as it refuses to suggest the role of unschooled students to be patronized. It invites readers to participate in the movement of the speaker-poet's own consciousness, as the lover who is addressed in the poem is invited to do. There's an intimacy in the poet's relationship with her readers; she establishes an identification with us, inviting us to participate in the poem, even as she demands our effort, our openness, and our commitment.

—Jenny Goodman, "Politics and the Personal Lyric in the Poetry of Joy Harjo and C. D. Wright," *MELUS* 19, no. 2 (Summer 1994): 42–44

Several notions of narrative and storytelling operate in Harjo's poetry. Several types of borders are crossed. Storytelling proclaims different functions. In his essay, "Native American Oral Narratives: Context and Continuity," Kenneth Roemer (1983:45–46) describes a storyteller: "A good storyteller uses his body and his voice. . . . old Cheyenne storytellers began their sacred narratives by smoothing the ground and going through a brief ritual of making the dirt and touching their bodies." This act of smoothing the earth signified that the Creator made humans and the earth, and that the Creator was now witnessing this story. The storyteller ceremonially crosses the boundaries between the earth and humans by touching the soil of the earth to her body, for the Creator to see her tell the story. Such accounts of Native storytellers validate the idea that storytelling is a performance, that there are actions and consequences to consider. In an interview Harjo discussed energy, power, and action of stories: "We all felt the energy—after the trading of stories, and hearing the stories—the power of those stories. Many of them included torture, destruction, torture, destruction, over and over. And stories of survival" ⟨Helen Jaskoski, "A MELUS Interview," 1989, 9⟩. The act of torture results in destruction, but the people survive as long as the stories are told, acted, performed.

Storytellers learn their stories from other storytellers and from experience. Their stories change with the speaker and with time and with circumstance. Each story is told from a subject-position which affects the telling of the story. In Harjo's book, *Secrets from the Center of the World*, co-authored with Stephen Strom, she writes of the "earth spirit" as the storyteller (Harjo and Strom 1989:54):

> Don't bother the earth spirit who lives here. She is working on a
> story. It is the oldest story in the world and it is delicate, changing. If
> she sees you watching she will invite you in for coffee, give you
> warm bread, and you will be obligated to stay and listen. But this is
> no ordinary story. You will have to endure earthquakes, lightning, the
> deaths of all those you love, the most blinding beauty. It's a story so
> compelling you may never want to leave; this is how she traps you.

Here the subject-position from which this story is being told is that of the earth spirit. The story she tells is delicate and changing, so the speaker and the listener are both operating tactically, in a shifting environment. When the earth spirit invites you in for coffee, she takes the listener into her home— includes him/her in the "homeplace" bell hooks speaks of. And if her story makes you never want to leave, perhaps that effect is the function of the earth spirit's narrative.

In another excerpt from the same book, Harjo's speaker describes stories as a storage site, a place with boundaries in which wealth can accumulate:

> Stories are our wealth. Winter nights we tell them over and over. Once a star fell from the sky, but it wasn't just any star, just as this isn't just any ordinary place. That cedar tree marks the event and the land remembers the flash of its death flight. To describe anything in winter whether it occurs in the past or the future requires a denser language, one thick with the promise of new lambs, heavy with the weight of corn milk. (Harjo and Strom 1989:24)

While such a site for accumulation of wealth would imply definite boundaries, and thus strategic operations, the notion that a language can be "thick with the promise of new lambs" and "heavy with the weight of corn milk," implies a disregard for boundaries between language and nature, or text and nature. Thus, such a disregard for boundaries would point toward tactical operations. Additionally, the reference to the "we" that tells stories over and over, implies a multiple subject-position. And the idea that this "isn't just any ordinary place," suggests another viewpoint for hook's "homeplace" (a place to grow and develop and nurture our spirits) and ⟨Michel⟩ de Certeau's "everyday" (a place where subjects operate tactically to invent themselves).

    —Mary Leen, "An Art of Saying: Joy Harjo's Poetry and the Survival of Storytelling," *American Indian Quarterly* 19, no. 1 (Winter 1995): 5–6

SANDRA M. GILBERT

A ⟨. . .⟩ yearning for ancient, soon-to-be-lost ways of speaking "cherishing and farewell" pervades Joy Harjo's *The Woman Who Fell from the Sky*. A member of the Creek tribe, Harjo performs her work on an audiocassette packaged with this book and draws heavily on Native American traditions throughout the volume, as she did in her four earlier collections. "I believe that the word poet is synonymous with the word truth teller," she explains, "so this collection tells a bit of the truth of what I have seen since my coming of age in the late sixties." These truths are notably shaped, however, by the "Mothertongue" of Harjo's culture, so that both narratives of memory and fantasies of desire are embodied in magical, sometimes surrealistic prose tales or long lines of incantatory, often ritualistic verse.

    The Woman Who Fell from the Sky opens, for example, with a moving elegy for Audre Lorde entitled "Reconciliation: A Prayer," and includes as well as a number of poems of naming, praising, and mourning for the writer's family and friends. Intermittently, in swift imaginative leaps, Harjo evokes legendary realms where gods and ancestors uttered primordial words and "Myth was as real as a scalp being scraped for lice." Thus "Reconciliation" begins with a god "lonely for touch" who "imagined herself as a woman, with children to suckle, to sing with—to continue the web of the terrifyingly beautiful cosmos of her womb" and concludes with a ceremonial invocation "of the four directions" commonly called upon in Native American prayers, spells, and blessings:

Of the south, where we feasted and were given new clothes.

Of the west, where we gave up the best of us to the stars as food for
the battle.

Of the north, where we cried because we were forsaken by our
dreams.

Of the east because returned to us is the spirit of all that we love.

Similarly, the book's title poem is an originatory tale of a transformative
encounter between "Johnny" (who renames himself "Saint Coincidence") and
"Lila" (who becomes the mysterious woman who fell from the sky [and] was
neither a murderer nor a saint"):

> She was rather ordinary, though beautiful in her walk, like one who
> has experienced freedom from earth's gravity. When I see her I think
> of an antelope grazing the alpine meadows in mountains whose
> names are as ancient as the sound that created the first world.

"Like the sun falling in the west," the poet tells us, this mythic "event car-
ried particles of light through the trees" although it takes place just in front of
a very *verismo* Safeway, where Johnny has "made a turn from borrowing spare
change from strangers."

Through such juxtapositions of the ordinary and the extraordinary, Harjo
consistently questions our modern western categories of the "real" and the
"surreal." At the same time, her determination to ground the apparently fantastic in the supposedly quotidian validates the legitimacy of both even while
the italicized commentaries that she appends to each of her formal texts provide contextual explanation for what might otherwise baffle readers who don't
share her background. In "The Naming," for example, a "realistic" portrait of
her mother's mother follows a vividly visionary account of how the "night after
my granddaughter-born-for-only-son climbed from the underworld we could
smell ozone over the lake made of a few centuries of rain." And a brief discussion of "Bell's theorem which states that all actions have a ripple effect in this
world" glosses the luminously lovely "Insomnia and the Seven Steps to Grace"
which begins among celestial dream-figures and ends on the streets of Tucson:

> At dawn the panther of the heavens peers over the edge of the world.
> She hears the stars gossip with the sun, sees the moon washing her
> lean darkness with water electrified by prayers. All over the world
> there are those who can't sleep, those who never awaken.

My granddaughter sleeps on the breast of her mother with milk on her mouth. A fly contemplates the sweetness of lactose.

Her father is wrapped in the blanket of nightmares. For safety he approaches the red hills near Thoreau. They recognize him and sing for him.

Her mother has business in the house of chaos. She is a prophet disguised as a young mother who is looking for a job. She appears at the door of my dreams and we put the house back together . . . .

It's October, though the season before dawn is always winter. On the city streets of this desert town lit by chemical yellow travelers search for home.

At times, especially in the editorial passages scattered throughout the book, Harjo lapses into sentimentality or sententiousness as when, for example, in her comment on the title poem she declares about "this beloved planet we call home," that "I understood love to be the very gravity holding each leaf, each cell this earthy star together." Mostly, however, her investigations of memory and desire, of cherishing and farewell, are marked by powerful perceptions along with an urgent eloquence ⟨. . . .⟩

    —Sandra M. Gilbert, "Looks of Memory and Desire," *Poetry* 168, no. 5 (August 1996): 290–93

B I B L I O G R A P H Y

The Last Song. 1975.

What Moon Drove Me to This? 1979.

She Had Some Horses. 1983.

Secrets from the Center of the World (with Stephen Strom). 1989.

In Mad Love and War. 1990.

Fishing. 1992.

The Woman Who Fell from the Sky. 1994.

Reinventing the Enemy's Language: Contemporary Native Women's Writing of North America (editor). 1997.

LINDA HOGAN

B. 1947

BORN IN COLORADO in 1947, Linda Hogan is a member of the Chickasaw tribe. Although as a child she spent time in Germany, when her father was stationed there as a member of the military, she has lived most of her life in Colorado and Oklahoma, which would become the central landscapes in her fiction, poetry, and essays. From her family Linda first heard the history of the Chickasaw tribe; even as a child, she was aware that her history as a Native American was missing from the textbooks and thus needed to be saved and remembered.

Hogan did not, however, grow up intending to be a writer; she did not start writing until she was in her 20s and went on to receive a master's degree in creative writing from the University of Colorado in 1978. She says that her poetry initially met with resistance because it did not conform to what people expected from "Indian poetry." In order to find her own voice, she had to "find her own teachers," as she puts it, and insist to others (and to herself) that the Native experience was worth writing about. The authors Meridel LeSueur and Tillie Olsen, among others, helped Hogan refine her ideas about how to unify politics and creativity.

Now Hogan's political commitments—to women, to Native peoples, to the environment—reveal themselves clearly, but not didactically, in everything she writes. Her first collection of poems, *Calling Myself Home* (1978), for example, uses memory and personal experience to reflect on what she calls the "dissonance" between her own background and the dominant culture of the United States. Like many other Native writers, both male and female, Hogan's work reflects the cultural confusion of Indians in the late 20th century as they search for an authentic place for themselves, their heritage, and their future. Her fiction challenges stereotypical portrayals of Native women and the romanticized representations of Native cultures, particularly spirituality, and she is careful to point out that there is not a monolithic "Native American" culture but a wide range of social systems from tribe to tribe. The tendency to collapse distinctions between tribes into one romantic image is particularly seductive, she says; writing against that seductive image is central to her project and to her own survival as a Chickasaw woman in America. In this sentiment Hogan echoes what many other Native American writers have said: that writing and teaching are crucial to their own identity and to the preservation of Native American histories and cultures.

Linda Hogan is the recipient of many awards, including a 1986 National Endowment for the Arts grant for fiction and a Guggenheim Fellowship.

C R I T I C A L   E X T R A C T S

ANDREW WIGET

⟨Like Paula Gunn Allen, Joy Harjo, and Wendy Rose, also⟩ deeply concerned with her identity as a woman is Linda Hogan (Chickasaw). Her first book, *Calling Myself Home* (1978), centers on remembering as an act of love. The opening poem, "Turtle," transforms dreaming into a waking to consciousness of women who, with the shells of ages on their backs, can "see the years / back through his [turtle's] eyes." In the languid rhythms of dream speech and the discontinuity of associated images, she suggests the transformation of persons not only into animals but into aspects of the earth such as trees, clay, and sedimentary rock. She personifies the ambiguity of her state's name—Oklahoma is a Choctaw word that can mean both "red earth" and "red people"—in the image of a potter whose fingers absorbed the red clay from their impress upon the shape emerging at his wheel. But she also knows that her tribal name means "they left as a tribe not a very great while ago" and adds, "they are always leaving, those people." In that poem she bears witness to having to carry her heritage, her earth, her family entirely in her body. As the ambiguity of the title marvelously suggests, without a home she longs for one, to call herself back to Oklahoma and that past, but she realizes that in the end she can only, like the turtle, call her self home.

In *Daughters, I Love You* (1981) she continues to explore many of these themes under the shadow of a mushrooming pillar of fire, writing poetry in the face of nuclear holocaust. Less protest than plea, the many strong poems in this volume again exploit ironies of transformation: that light should be a sign of death and moral darkness; that mothers should be mourners giving birth to the doomed; that invention is destruction. The most potent irony: that all that women have come to symbolize for her—the earth, the future, the bond of shared humanity, the promise of continuance as a species—should be jeopardized in the name scrawled on the fuselage of the Hiroshima-bound B-29; "The Enola Gay, / was named for the pilot's mother."
—Andrew Wiget, *Native American Literature* (Boston: Twayne Publishers, 1985), 119

LYNDA KOOLISH

Transformation, fantasy, and dream-vision are ⟨. . .⟩ crucial to Native American poet Linda Hogan's "Wall Songs," a poem of astonishingly lovely lyricism and enormous shamanistic power. The speaker in the poem names that fragile covering of the body, her skin, as "the real life / of love and sorrow," thus affirming sexuality and the physical apprehension of a beloved as crucial to the deepest levels of emotional understanding. The walls here are material and actual: roads which separate jungles, wire fences, ledges "embedded with green / and broken glass." In the face of the things which divide us (race, class, and sexual preference), in the face of danger and violence, "the singing of machetes," the speaker utters a prayer for healing, for the dissolution of boundaries—geographical, physical, and those of the heart. A priestess, a shaman, she claims the terrain of the body and the cartography of compassion, friendship, sexuality, and love as a force to transform divisions into bridges, to create a community, a world at peace:

> . . . Sometimes a lover
> and I turn our flesh to bridges
> and the air between us disappears
> like in the jungle
> where I am from.
> Tropical vines grow together, lovers,
> over roadways men have slashed,
> surviving
> the sounds of those lost inside
> and the singing of machetes.
>
> May all walls be like those of the jungle,
> filled with animals
> singing into the ears of night.
> Let them be
> made of the mysteries further in
> in the heart, joined with the lives of all,
> all bridges of flesh,
> all singing,
> all covering the wounded land
> showing again, again
> that boundaries are all lies. ⟨Seeing through the Sun, 1985, 67–68⟩

—Lynda Koolish, "The Bones of This Body Say, Dance: Self-Empowerment in Contemporary Poetry by Women of Color," in A Gift of Tongues: Critical Challenges in Contemporary American Poetry, ed. Marie Harris and Kathleen Aguero (Athens, GA: The University of Georgia Press, 1987), 32–33

BO SCHÖLER

⟨Interview with Linda Hogan by Bo Schöler⟩

LH: It's becoming easier for me to say things and take certain risks. I'm becoming more verbal. I'm becoming more capable of using language. Being a person who didn't read, writing has opened new possibilities for me. And, as a writer, my language has changed. I write differently here, in this environment, than I did in a quiet environment. The book *Eclipse* is a book that's written in silence and in the natural world. *Seeing Through The Sun* and the book I'm working on now are books that are written in places where buses pass by. There's a difference in the language. I'm speeded up here.

BS: In terms of storytelling, it seems to me that what you're trying to do is recreate ethnic history in your book *That Horse*. And it's something that you do much more in your fiction than in your poetry. Are you trying to recreate ethnic history?

LH: In *That Horse*, my father's story and my story are about the same horse, but they're very different stories. I wanted to show the history of the time. I don't know if it's ethnic history, or if it's the history of that particular place and the people in that place. My father's story was personal. I wanted to expand his story to show the historical circumstances, but I also wanted my grandfather in there. He was a bronc-rider, and that interests me. But the other stories in *That Horse* are a straightforward telling of stories. I think "Amen" has a lot to do with Christianity and the influence it has and doesn't have over people in that area. A friend of mine was talking about how she thinks the last vestiges of older tradition are found in the Christian churches. When you sing "Amazing Grace" in Chickasaw, that's everything we've ever been that still exists. But while Christianity has been destructive for the tribes, it still holds people together. In "Amen" I wanted to write about the lake that my father worked on. "Crow" is a straightforward, contemporary story. I'm tired of reading stories about Indian people that don't seem to me to be true: no bumperstickers, no events going on. ⟨. . .⟩

I'm careful about what I write. I don't want to hurt or alienate anyone, but I feel there are some things that have to be said. When Gertrude Bonnin Simmons wrote about the young Indian men who went to college, returned and sold out their own people, cheated elderly people off the land, I'm sure she was unpopular for speaking it, but she told the truth. I want to write about young men here who get their grandmas' welfare checks and use it all up and leave their grandmas in the city without any money. That's also the truth.

Those things need to be said. There's a Brazilian woman who kept journals—Carolina Maria de Jesus—and she began to publish them. She told people she was going to tell on them, she was going to write about them if they beat up their wives. And so they didn't.

BS: Does feedback influence the way you write?

LH: Sometimes I think, "Why do I write? Why don't I just go . . . be?" I often think I'm the kind of person that would like to live out in the middle of nowhere, and just take care of whatever needs to be taken care of, to live and sit around and stare at the hills, and explore the land and the stars. And I do that from time to time. For long periods of time I'm a person who loves to sit. But when I go to a conference for Indian women and I'm sitting in the audience and one of the speakers says, "There's Linda Hogan, the poet, and we're so proud that Indian women are doing these things," it keeps me going. I realize then, that when we get to see our real life written down in words, it feeds us.

> —Bo Schöler, "A Heart Made out of Crickets: An Interview with Linda Hogan," *The Journal of Ethnic Studies* 16, no. 1 (Spring 1988): 113–16

CAROL MILLER

⟨Interview with Linda Hogan by Carol Miller⟩

CM: One of the things I admired about your book ⟨*Mean Spirit*⟩ was that it was historical. And a point that has been made about fiction written by people of color is that almost no one has been able to deal with historical reality in fictional form. There's been a lot of contemporary writing, but the iniquity and the pain and the suffering that people went through historically is just not accessible yet. The exception I was thinking of might be Toni Morrison's *Beloved*, and your novel is the other example of an attempt to get at that historical material. Were you intimidated? Did you even think abut it? Did you choose because the story was so strong, rather than choosing, say, a contemporary story?

LH: Well, I knew this story forward and back, top to bottom, and I needed to tell it. It's as if the story chose me instead of me choosing the story. Every time I turned around another piece of it would pop up. One time I went to a ceremony and there was a woman there who told me that she was from Osage County, an older woman, and she added a facet to the story. It's been that way throughout the whole process, through the years I've worked on it and those earlier years of preparation for it before I even knew it was there, that every time I turn around I'm being shown some other part of it.

CM: My special interest is in the story-telling traditions, and I wondered as I read the book and as I read your poetry and Erdrich and Silko and others, I wondered if the story-telling tradition was as potent for you in your background, in your practice, as those writers have said it is for them.

LH: I never really know what that means—"story-telling tradition"—because I think the picture that brings to mind is this sort of old-time person sitting around a bunch of little kids gesturing with his hands. It's always a "him," telling stories of myth, of creation, or coyote stories or something. So, if that's what you mean, no, I didn't have that in my life as a child, and I don't think very many people really do, particularly where we're from. But, my dad was a story-teller, a great story-teller. It's so amazing to me to listen because he makes a complete sentence verbally. He doesn't say "uh" or "um" like most of us do. He just speaks straight out, plain and clear. And he's very visual. The people in my family who tell stories in that way are very imagistic. Also like my Uncle Wesley would say—everybody in my dad's family were all musicians—he'd say he couldn't read any music. It looked like a bunch of blackbirds sitting on a telephone line. So they always had a way to illustrate the story—the thing that they were saying was really visual—and give examples.

And they all talked about history. They talked about our pasts and when I was young I'd write down everything that they said because I knew, I always felt from the very beginning . . . I knew there was a history to our life that needed to be saved, a history not in books or films. You know, Scott Momaday says that the oral tradition is one generation away from extinction always, and while I don't know if what my dad and family and my grandmother spoke was what you would call the oral tradition, I knew that they were important stories and that they had to be documented. It's our lives.

—Carol Miller, "The Story is Brimming Around: An Interview with Linda Hogan," *Studies in American Indian Literatures* 2, no. 4 (Winter 1990): 4–5

CRAIG WOMACK

Linda Hogan uses primordial images in her poems in *Calling Myself Home*: red clay, insects, turtles, light, water, organs. These images, like the dancing light of fireflies on a humid summer evening, flicker and flit in and out of the poetry and stories, appearing throughout the book. Hogan is concerned with the home one physically inhabits and the home one holds in the imagination, and home is shown to be a spiritual process of growing connection to place rather than a static location. ⟨. . . T⟩he clay forms the poet: "These first poems were part of that return for me, an identification with my tribe and the Oklahoma earth, a deep knowing and telling how I was formed of these two powers called ancestors and clay . . . In these poems live red land and light" (p. 1).

Turtles are dominant in Hogan's poetry, appropriately enough since these animals are central to the lives of traditional Southeastern tribeswomen. Women fashion shell-shakers from turtles and wear them on their legs during stomp dances. Anyone who has heard the *shuguta shuguta* sound of pebbles shaking in the shells on the legs of women dancing counter-clockwise around the fire cannot forget these women moving over the earth, shaking out their rhythms. Turtle inhabits dual worlds: he goes into the water and emerges again on land, making him especially powerful. The turtle, in spite of his hard ossified covering, internally, is soft with the "small yellow bones of animals inside" (p. 5). Women shell shakers pull apart these hard shells and expose the soft parts, cleaning them out before making their rattles. Hogan calls for a similar exposure:

> We should open his soft parts,
> pull his shells apart
> and wear them on our backs
> like old women who can see the years
> back through his eyes.
>
> Something is breathing in there.
> Wake up, we are women.
> The shells are on our backs.
> We are amber,
> the small animals
> are gold inside us. (p. 5)

The suggestion that the past can be seen through the eyes of the turtle and the contrast between inside and outside is Hogan's exhortation to women who have the potential to carry within themselves the entirety of their cultures through their power to imagine and speak the past. Like turtle who moves between land and water, they can creatively move between past and present, using those who have come before as guides for contemporary experience. ⟨. . .⟩

The poetry in the collection is more memorable than the prose selections. The prose, however, is introduced with background essays that contain interesting anecdotes about the evolution of the stories and some pithy wisdom. For instance, in the introduction to "The Black Horse," Hogan says, "Fiction clarifies the world without muddling life with the bias of fact" (p. 41). The author is a talented essayist, and it is unfortunate that some of her creative nonfiction is not included in another section of the book. One of the singular prose stories, "Amen," features a one-eyed character named Jack; i.e., a one-eyed Jack, who, like turtle, enters the water and later emerges from it, in an act that becomes embedded in the people's memories and stories. The story has a mythical quality; Jack's swim occurs on the "night of the big fish" when the men of the community catch a large one-eyed fish, so big that one of them hollers "I could put my hands in that gill slit" (p. 67). An observer of these events who enters the water with Jack and later comes back out, traversing worlds like turtle also, is the young woman Sullie. She, and the rest of the community are renewed through partaking of the flesh of the fish which is closely associated with Jack. The story, with its poetic connections, is haunting and stays with the reader for a long time. Some of the other stories lack the same amount of development.

—Craig Womack, [Review of *Red Clay: Poems and Stories*], *The American Indian Quarterly* 17, no. 1 (Winter 1993): 104–5

ROBERT L. BERNER

Linda Hogan, who is of mixed Chickasaw and European ancestry, is one of a handful of the most important poets of American Indian background among the many writing today. In her previous collections she has demonstrated an ability to relate Indian realities to the universality of what makes us human, and though some of the poems in *Savings* (1988; see *WLT* 63:4, p. 723) may have seemed somewhat political, they avoided ideological pitfalls and their images were drawn from the most basic elements of the natural world. It is the latter concern which is most apparent in her preoccupation with nature's most primordial elements in *The Book of Medicines*.

Many of the poems are populated with animals, seen in startling images that capture the naked power of the natural world: a mountain lion frightened by the wild human animal it confronts, a fetal whale floating on a block of ice, a crow and wolf scavenging the body of a fallen moose. Images of this kind often give us the sense of being present at the creation of the world—"I remember / . . . when whales lived on land / and we stepped out of water / to enter our lives in air" ("Crossings")—or at least at the beginning of human culture, as in a poem about a hibernating bear killed in its den by starving hunters and by dogs which are themselves still almost wolves ("Bear Fat").

The Book of Medicines includes so many fine things that a choice of examples is not easy. Three seem to me to be characteristic. In "The Alchemists" the ancient effort to transmute lead into gold becomes a metaphor for the act of the physician attempting to change sickness into health: "A man . . . willing iron to be gold. / If it had worked / we would kneel down before it / and live forever, / all base metals / in ceremonial fire." "The Fallen" combines images of a meteorite fallen to earth and a starving pregnant wolf caught in a trap to produce a terrifying vision. The traditional (presumably Chickasaw) myth of the Great Wolf as a constellation that was "the mother of all women" is contrasted with the sterility of modern science, defined in relation to the myth of Lucifer, the light-bringer and devil, and the narrator's inability to throw the fallen stone back into the sky produces a final frightening vision of science and technology as a trapper/wolf destroying the natural world. And in "Tear" the traditional "tear" dresses of Chickasaw women and a racial memory of the sad march of the Chickasaws to Oklahoma are combined to produce a powerful affirmation of the poet's own identity both as descendant and ancestor: "I am why they survived. / The world behind them did not close. / The world before them is still open. / All around me are my ancestors, / my unborn children."

The Book of Medicines is a significant step, indeed a giant stride, in the development of a major American poet.

—Robert L. Berner, [Review of Book of Medicines], World Literature Today 68, no. 2 (Spring 1994): 407–8

MARC H. STEINBERG

How wealthy were Oklahoma's Osage Indians in the 1920s as depicted in Linda Hogan's novel Mean Spirit (NY: Ivy, 1988)? They were well enough off that their multiple automobile purchases and frivolous, excessive spending is far from exaggerated. The oil boom peaked in 1922 and 1923, the time frame of the novel, and white men were eager to encroach on the Indians' valuable land. And, although they were abused on many levels (including the momentary and physical) because of whites' insatiable hunger for riches, the average Osage family of five at that time "had an income of $65,000 a year" (Science, Apr. 1980:32–35).

Hogan de-emphasizes the role of money in the lives of Indians because, as a matter of fact and of spiritual tradition, it was not a revered possession. The Osages did not inhabit by choice the oil-rich territory of northeastern Oklahoma; rather, they were forced in the late 19th century to migrate south from Kansas. This passage provided a mixed blessing—true, oil was discovered on their reservation in 1897; but some twenty years later "murders and elaborate confidence schemes were uncovered [and] white men married Osage women for control" [Terry P. Wilson, The Underground Reservation: Osage Oil (Lincoln: Univ. of Nebraska Press, 1985, xi)]. The multiple murders in Mean Spirit point to the greed of the white men; plotting was wide-spread and conspiratorial, involving a police chief as well as a rancher turned oil tycoon;

and there is even the suggestion that the murders may have been directed by much higher sources, the operators of Federal agencies. After several persons were convicted in 1926, including the novel's main villain, William Hale (named John Hale by Hogan), the reign of terror effectively came to an end. While the novel concentrates on several murders, in fact there were as many as twenty.

More important than the lawlessness of the whites ⟨and⟩ the excessiveness of the Osages, Hogan vividly describes a tribe of spiritual people who disregarded wealth because, in comparison with their relationship with nature and each other, monetary riches were valueless. Readers should keep in mind that traditional tribal values were often in direct contrast with urban industrial values. While the urban concentrated on competition, taking, saving, and the future, the Indian focused on coalition, donation, sharing, and the present. Hence money was not so highly regarded.

Several whites in the novel reject their culture and develop Indian mannerisms and styles; by so doing, Martha Billy and China come to an awareness of the value of the Osage tribe. While "most of the Indian people lost trust in the whites" (170), some whites also lost trust in the whites. But, on another level—that of monetary wealth—whites cannot trust Indians, for Indians do not know the "value" of money and, consequently, cannot be sane. A number of the Indians are deemed "incompetent" and given guardians to manage their money. The whites think that it can be nothing short of insane for Grace Blanket (the first victim) to purchase a grand piano and let it rot in her yard, or for Indians to buy expensive Buicks and trade them for near worthless items. Historically, "in one case, an Indian went through ten cars in 1 year" (*Science* 33). Does this behavior signify incompetence? Not if one is aware that for most tribal members, at least in the 1920s, money was paper and paper, in itself, was valueless. Consequently, the money had to be spent on items which, in themselves, could be of great or minor value to the Indians and whose value had little to do with price tags.

Near the conclusion of *Mean Spirit*, Lettie, who has suffered from the murders of her husband, family, and friends, is pleased with her inheritance—"the feather of Osage Star-Looking . . . the only thing I ever wanted passed down to me" (368). What the Osages inherited could not be reduced to monetary terms; they inherited wild horses, bees, owls, cornfields, caves, symbols, and icons, things for which they were held just as responsible as were the whites for their material wealth.

—Marc H. Steinberg, "Linda Hogan's *Mean Spirit*: The Wealth, Value, and Worth of the Osage Tribe," *Notes on Contemporary Literature* 25, no. 2 (March 1995): 7–8

B I B L I O G R A P H Y

Calling Myself Home. 1978.
Daughters, I Love You. 1981.
Eclipse. 1983.
That House. 1985.
Seeing through the Sun. 1985.
Savings: Poem. 1988.
Mean Spirit. 1990.
Red Clay: Poems and Stories. 1991.
Book of Medicines. 1993.
Dwellings: A Spiritual History of the Living World. 1995.
Solar Storms. 1995.

E. PAULINE JOHNSON
1861–1913

KNOWN ALSO AS Tekahionwake, Emily Pauline Johnson was born in 1861 in Ontario to a Mohawk father and an English mother who was cousin to the American author W. D. Howells. She was raised on the Six Nations Reservation, where she learned Mohawk history from her paternal grandfather and English poetry from her mother; deeply inspired by both, she herself began writing poems in her teens. Johnson's later poetry and short stories would reflect her complex heritage. Her career as a writer would always be dependent upon her career as a performer, and this too reflected her dual heritage: she gave public poetry recitations as "The Mohawk Princess," wearing a buckskin dress for half the evening and changing into a ball gown for the other half.

Johnson's recitations preceded the publication of her work, and she said that she gave her performances—which were extremely popular—in order to earn the money to travel to England, where she hoped to find a publisher for her poetry manuscript. In 1884 she left for England, and amid much social success she had her manuscript, *The White Wampum,* accepted by the Bodley Head press. The book was not actually released until 1895, however, by which point Johnson had returned to Canada; she immediately set out on a performance tour to promote the book. Although the volume received mixed reviews, Johnson kept writing, both poetry and short stories.

Many of Johnson's short stories were published in popular magazines of the day, like *Mother's Magazine* and *Boy's World.* The stories are romantic and Victorian in their sensibilities: their heroines are usually beautiful, moral, mixed-blood Indian maidens, and the settings are often picturesque, "primitive" villages. But Johnson does attempt to avoid other stereotypes of Native Americans by giving her characters moral and spiritual dilemmas and by asserting the importance of family and home as the bedrock of the Indian community.

Johnson's semiautobiographical book, *The Moccasin Maker,* was published posthumously in 1913 and was intended to include stories of the Six Nations. Because Johnson died before she could record these, the published volume contains essays and short stories, most of which focused on women. In some of these stories, Johnson becomes slightly more polemical than in her earlier stories: the character sketch "My Mother," for instance, examines Johnson's politically active grandmother, and the short story "As It Was in the Beginning" uncovers the racism and sexism of many Christian values.

Johnson continued writing and performing until her death from breast cancer in 1913. As testimony to her popularity as an entertainer, she was given a civic funeral in Vancouver, where she was mourned by thousands of those who remembered "The Mohawk Princess."

CRITICAL EXTRACTS

BETTY KELLER

It was not until July 1895 that *The White Wampum* was finally released. By this time, Pauline had almost despaired of seeing it, but, though she was seething with frustration, there was little that she could do from Canada to speed the publishing process. And every month had brought new promises and new disappointments ⟨. . . .⟩

However, when the book finally appeared, Pauline's career received the boost she had been waiting for, because the reviewers sat up and paid attention. Virtually the earliest and best review was written by the critic for *The Week*. "We have read them all," said the reviewer, "—some more than once—and we have not found a bad or indifferent poem in the collection!" He remarked on the

> power of lucid, picturesque, forcible expression possessed by Miss Johnson. No one can fail to be struck with the musical rhythm of her lines, and she has great power of rhyming—no slight accomplishment, and one which we venture to think constitutes a very considerable ornament to English poetry. A good example of charming word painting—word music rather—is "The Song my Paddle Sings."

The reviews from Britain were mixed. From the *St. James Budget*, "Miss Johnson reaches a high level in both thought and expression in the later and more personal poems." *The Literary World* of London said:

> The authoress has no original way of wrapping her subjects up in words. She follows models that are not particularly deserving of the compliment that is implied by imitation. It is when she does not aim herself at the redskin, so to speak, that we like her most. When she is restful, she charms, and there are a few poems in this little book that deserve to be honoured by critics of all sorts and one of these is "Sunset." Another is "Overlooked."

The *Glasgow Herald* disagreed. "The best things in the book," they announced, "are some Indian tales which fairly breathe the spirit of the red-man and his home in the great forests and the illimitable prairie." The *Guardian*, unaware of her lineage, declared, "The idea of posing as an Indian bard cannot be counted among her happiest inspirations," but a week later another reviewer in the same paper decided that he quite liked her work. The *Pall Mall Gazette* was commendatory; the *Sketch* was ambivalent, and the *Westminster Gazette* could find nothing in the volume that it "would be doing justice to the writer to quote."

Pauline presumably suffered the usual pangs that a creator feels when his work is maligned or commended, but she has left only one comment. On the back of a clipping of a review that referred to her as a "Bostonian," she wrote: "God forgive the slanderers. Why, oh why am I called a Bostonian?"

—Betty Keller, *Pauline: A Biography of Pauline Johnson* (Vancouver: Douglas & McIntyre, 1981), 101–2

A. LaVonne Brown Ruoff

To dismiss E. Pauline Johnson's work as melodramatic romanticism designed to tug the heart strings of her audiences is to deny her impact as a performer and writer on the development of Canadian literature. Her hectic stage schedule and her need to write what could be sold or performed clearly inhibited her growth as a writer. Nevertheless, her works appealed to the fundamental emotions of her audiences, who viewed her not only as an author but also as a vibrant presence who could dramatize these emotions before their enraptured eyes. ⟨. . .⟩

Both as a performer and as a writer, Pauline is best known as an interpreter of the Indian to non-Indian audiences. ⟨Norman⟩ Shrive accurately describes her as "one of the few people who saw through the popular image of the Indian and who said so in writing" ⟨"What Happened to Pauline," 32⟩. During Pauline's lifetime the stereotype of the bloodthirsty savage was vividly reinforced in the public's mind by accounts of the Indian wars in the United States and by the mixed-blood rebellions led by Louis Riel in Canada (1869–70, 1884–85). Fears of Indian uprisings in the United States were fanned in 1890 by the Ghost Dance Movement that spread through Indian reservations and by the massacre at Wounded Knee.

To counteract the stereotypes of the "bloodthirsty savage" and the venial mixed blood, stock figures in the westerns of the period, Pauline creates idealized portraits of Indian and mixed-blood women who possess far more goodness and morality than do the whites who betray them or who are slow to recognize their virtues. However, as Shrive points out, Pauline ironically became part of the artificiality against which she protested in her writing.

Although she protested against stereotypical "noble Savages," she also used them in her work. For example, her young mixed-blood heroines are unfailingly beautiful, possessing the best qualities of both the red and white races. They also bear a marked physical resemblance to Pauline herself. Christine, the heroine of "A Red Girl's Reasoning," is described as looking "much the same as her sisters, all Canada through, who are the offspring of red and white parentage—olive-complexioned, gray-eyed, black-haired, with figure slight and delicate, and the wistful, unfathomable expression in her whole face that turns one so heart-sick as they glance at the young Indians of to-day—it is the forerunner too frequently of 'the white man's disease,' consumption. . ." ⟨The Moccasin Maker, 1987, 104⟩. The heroine of "The Derelict" possesses similar physical characteristics: ". . . a type of mixed blood, pale, dark, slender, with the slim hands, the marvelously beautiful teeth of her mother's people, the ambition, the small tender mouth, the utter fearlessness of the English race. But the strange, laughless eyes, the silent step, the hard sense of honor, proclaimed her far more a daughter of red blood than of white" (213). Pauline's mixed-blood heroines are unfailingly loyal to the men they love until betrayed. Her Indian mothers are virtuous to a fault. However, the situations in which Pauline involves her heroines are real, and she attempts to make her heroines reflect their tribal heritages, rather than relying, as did most non-Indian authors, on artificial creations that owe more to Chateaubriand's *Atala* than to existing Indian cultures.

— A. LaVonne Brown Ruoff, "Introduction" to *The Moccasin Maker* by E. Pauline Johnson (Tucson: The University of Arizona Press, 1987), 31–33

George W. Lyon

That Johnson should have identified herself with nature is no surprise. Sherry Ortner has called our attention to a widespread tendency to view culture as the masculine domain and achievement and nature, that environment which must be tamed by culture, as feminine. Pauline Johnson was twice attached to nature: as a woman and as a native. ⟨Terry⟩ Goldie's comments on the indigene and nature echo comparisons by Ortner, ⟨R. A.⟩ Sydie, and others on woman and nature:

> It would be possible to divide much of the semiosis of our society, if not all, between the semiotic fields of nature and art. That part of our environment which is not shaped by man and that which is . . . . The indigence is often used to present the possibility of nature in a human form. In the same way, the indigene's closeness to nature is used to justify an emphasis on the indigene as land. ⟨*Fear and Temptation*, 1989, 19⟩

Remembering that Goldie identifies the Indian woman figure as Temptress, we should add to this Sydie's comment, "It is not simply that nature, 'like' women, is to be subject to mastery but also that nature, again like women, is understood as a mysterious, unpredictable and, therefore, dangerous Other" ⟨*Natural Women, Cultured Women*, 1987, 205⟩. If that "dangerous Other" reminds us of Northrup Frye's "alien continent" by which one is "silently swallowed", Goldie finds that the Princess/Temptress offers more than a carnival for the European libido,

> She represents the attractions of the land but in a form which seems
> to request domination, unlike her violent male counterpart who
> resists it. The image of the female as the receiver of the male power
> provides an explicit opportunity for the white patriarchy to enter the
> land. If . . . the sexual relationship is repressed or even denied she
> becomes still more explicitly object, as the domination is not through
> sexual 'interaction' but through the spectator-owner. And at all times
> she represents a passionate heterosexuality with the limited perver-
> sion of miscegenation—with all the tensions that, as Foucault shows,
> are productive of discourse. (65–66)

Goldie implicates Pauline Johnson at every turn. Not only could a sexual relationship with her result in miscegenation, she herself was the product of miscegenation. The allure of that "limited perversion," from the half-castes of the Raj to the quadroons of New Orleans, has been the subject of many discourses, from Noel Coward to Tennessee Williams. The dominant gaze of the spectator-owner was as much a part of her costumed readings as of a stripshow. The stage produces and thrives upon repressed, or at least postponed, sexuality. And repressed or thwarted sexuality ⟨. . .⟩ formed a great deal of her content. In the case of "Ojistoh," particularly, revenge involved sexual arousal, quite possibly arousal of repressed disloyalty to patriarchy, if the narrator's admiration for the Huron is not entirely feigned. One wonders whether or not Johnson in her single-driver canoes did not project the sort of vulnerability that made Marilyn Monroe seem as accessible as she was attractive. Such would have constituted a clear invitation to enter, inhabit, nourish (as Foucault speaks of the nourishing state), and dominate the land. It is perhaps not surprising, then, that ⟨Marcus⟩ Van Steen writes of Johnson visiting." . . . remote communities [which were, after all, at the leading edge of the domination] like a vigorous and refreshing wind from civilization, bringing not only entertainment but a vision of Canada stretching from sea to sea" ⟨*Pauline Johnson*, 1965, 26⟩. Roy Daniells finds in Johnson's Indian poems "the intimacy between Indian life and western landscape" and in Johnson herself "a symbol which satisfies a felt need . . . to realize topography in terms of life . . . the fundamental fact of Canadian experience" ⟨"Minor Poets," 1967, 442⟩. Two years after Johnson's death, J. D. Robins wrote of "the weird and fascinating legends of the soil . . . whose spirit breathes so strongly and beautifully through the work of Pauline Johnson. Of these we are the sole heirs . . ." ⟨"Backgrounds of Future Canadian Poetry," 1975, 141⟩. If Johnson's assignment was to tame nature and to pass it on to a white patriarchy, she seems to have succeeded.

—George W. Lyon, "Pauline Johnson: A Reconsideration," *Studies in Canadian Literature* 15, no. 2 (1990): 150–52

A. LaVonne Brown Ruoff

"Red Girl's Reasoning" was one of the most popular works in Johnson's performance repertory. Awarded the 1892 first prize for fiction by *Dominion Magazine*, the story was published in the journal's February 1893 issue (2:1, pp. 19–28). Although she talked about turning it into a play, Johnson never did. Central issues in this story are white refusal to accept the sanctity of the tribal marriage ceremonies of white men to Indian women and the independence of women. Johnson presents these issues through the plot of domestic romance, in which the heroine gains her goal of marriage. She departs from this pattern by having the heroine leave her husband in order to maintain her sense of virtue and self-worth as mixed-blood and as a woman. ⟨. . .⟩

Few women authors of the period broke this sharply with the domestic-romance formula. ⟨. . .⟩ ⟨A⟩lthough the new theme of the independent woman in American literature called for a new plot that would not "resistlessly flow to the magnetic terminal of marriage," the women writers of the nineties could not break free of the marriage pattern. They may have hinted at scrapping marriage or treating it as another episode in the continuing development of feminine self-awareness, yet they did not carry out such actions. In "Red Girl's Reasoning" Johnson stresses that when they choose marriage partners, Indian and mixed-blood women face dangers greater than those faced by white women. Even a partner from a good family who appears to be sympathetic to Indians while living in the bush can become an unfeeling tyrant who expresses the prejudices of the dominant society when he returns to civilization.

—A. LaVonne Brown Ruoff, "Justice for Indians and Women: The Protest Fiction of Alice Callahan and Pauline Johnson," *World Literature Today* 66, no. 2 (Spring 1992): 252–53

A. LaVonne Brown Ruoff

Johnson's finest lyrics are "Morrow Land," written at Easter 1900; "Heidelburgh" (originally titled "To C. W."); and "Song," all unpublished in her lifetime ⟨. . .⟩ "Heidelburgh" reveals powerful and bitter personal emotions not present in Johnson's earlier work. Her mature lyricism is exemplified in "Song":

> The night-long shadows faded into gray,
> Then silvered into glad and gold sunlight,
> Because you came to me, like a new day
> Born of the beauty of an autumn night.

The author's supporters collected her stories about women and her essay "A Pagan in St. Paul's Cathedral" as *The Moccasin Maker*, which was published posthumously in 1913. Like the heroines in most women's nineteenth-century fiction, the female protagonists of Johnson's stories inevitably triumph over great difficulty. They and their lovers recognize that genuine love between men and women reflects shared values. Johnson combines the domestic romance with protest literature, expressing her anger at the injustices experienced by women and Indians in "Red Girl's Reasoning" and "As It Was in the Beginning," two of the best stories in the collection. In both, she combines the plot of the mixed-blood woman betrayed by a weak white lover with a forceful attack on white religious hypocrisy. "The Legend of Lillooet Falls," "Tenas Klootchman," and "Catherine of the 'Crow's Nest'" depict the deep love Indian women feel for their natural and adopted children, as well as the roles they play as guardians of tribal traditions. Mother love is also a powerful force in Johnson's stories about white frontier women, such as "My Mother," a fictionalized account of her parents' courtship and marriage. In "A Pagan in St. Paul's Cathedral" Johnson draws parallels between Indian and white religions and concludes that the differences are unimportant.

Critics have had mixed reactions to Johnson's work. Although they have praised the lyricism of some of her poems, they also have noted her tendency to sentimentalism in her verse and her fiction. Many focused on the extent to which her Indian poetry was or was not authentic. Charles Mair, a Canadian poet and a friend of Johnson's, acclaimed her as one "'who spoke loud and bold,' not for the Iroquois alone, but for the whole red race, and sang of its glories and its wrongs in strains of poetic fire." The British critic Theodore Watts-Dunton saw her as representing an authentic Indian voice and predicted in his introduction to the 1913 edition of *Flint and Feather* that Johnson would hold a "memorable place among poets in virtue of her descent and also in virtue of the work she has left behind, small as the quantity of that work is." Johnson's reputation reached its zenith in the 1920s, when Canadian critics focused new attention on her generation of writers. The reaction against her poetry is voiced most forcefully by A. J. M. Smith, who argues that critics and journalists played up her Indian birth, which "has been accepted as convincing proof that she spoke with the authentic voice of the Red Man." Smith is unaware, however, that the poetry of many nineteenth- and turn-of-the-century Indian writers was strongly influenced by English and American romanticism.

—A. LaVonne Brown Ruoff, "E. Pauline Johnson (Tekahionwake)," *The Dictionary of Literary Biography* 175, ed. Kenneth M. Roemer (Detroit: Gale Research, 1997), 134–35

B I B L I O G R A P H Y

The White Wampum. 1895.
Canadian Born. 1903.
Legends of Vancouver. 1911.
The Moccasin Maker. 1913.
The Shagganappi. 1913.
Flint and Feather. 1917.

MOURNING DOVE
C. 1882–1936

MOURNING DOVE, or Humishuma, was born between 1882 and 1888 into an Okanogan family that bridged Indian and white cultures. Her father worked for wages in the white town where the family lived, at the same time continuing traditional food-gathering practices; Mourning Dove's mother enrolled her in a Catholic school but made sure that she learned traditional medicinal lore. Symbolic of this dual culture is the fact that Mourning Dove was also given an English name, Christine Quintasket, which is the name she used in her personal life. "Mourning Dove" was her pen name, under which she published the two works for which she is most famous: *Cogewea, the Half-Blood* (1927) and *Coyote Stories* (1933).

Mourning Dove, who is often considered the first Native American woman to publish a work of fiction in the United States, had perhaps only four years of elementary education and a year of typing school, in Canada. Her knowledge of published literature seems to have been limited to the popular novels of the period. One of these, Therese Broderick's *The Brand*, plays a role in Mourning Dove's own novel—as a symbol of the stereotypical images of the American Indian. *Cogewea*, in part, offers a revision of these stereotypical images. It is a mixture of fiction, Okanogan folktales, and details from Mourning Dove's own life. The conflicts faced by the central character, Cogewea, are those faced by Mourning Dove herself, as a Native woman in a non-Native culture. The first draft of the novel was finished in 1912, when Mourning Dove was living on the Flathead Reservation in northern Washington state, where she witnessed the last buffalo round-up, which she chronicles in Cogewea and describes as the "last link connecting the Indian to the past."

Mourning Dove met editor Lucullus McWhorter in 1914, and after the two became friends, she showed him the early manuscript of *Cogewea*. The critical issues surrounding the book center on the contribution by McWhorter, who, in addition to adding long ethnographic digressions and informational footnotes to educate the audience, is believed by some to have actually rewritten entire sections of the novel.

McWhorter seems not to have told Mourning Dove of the changes he made, and when, after years of struggle by both Mourning Dove and McWhorter, the novel was actually published, she wrote to McWhorter that she was "surprised" by the changes but also that she hoped "the general public will take that much interest in it and that would be fine." McWhorter's efforts on Mourning Dove's behalf seem motivated by his anger at the American government's treatment of Native Americans, and although Mourning Dove seems to have recognized that, in her second work, *Coyote Stories*, she was careful to limit McWhorter's involvement.

Coyote Stories is a collection of Okanogan legends and folktales, transcribed by Mourning Dove; she began writing down these tales—primarily genesis legends—because children were being taught to ridicule the stories of their own heritage. Her hope was that future generations would eventually be able to read these stories and thus be reconnected with their history.

Although Mourning Dove's work is not without flaw, it cleared the way for future generations of Native American writers, who would pick up on her themes of cultural confusion and hybridity, as well as her desire to celebrate and preserve tribal traditions.

CRITICAL EXTRACTS

MARY V. DEARBORN

It is impossible to be certain how much of *Co-ge-we-a* was written by Mourning Dove and how much by McWhorter. One charitable interpretation could conclude that McWhorter influenced Mourning Dove, making suggestions and editing heavily; at the other extreme an equally reasonable assessment could conclude that Mourning Dove talked and McWhorter wrote. There is simply too much in the novel for it to be the work of a single mind. Such speculation, however, obscures the real point, which is the way in which McWhorter translates, transcribes, and annotates the experience of Mourning Dove, and how each of them seems to have viewed their respective roles. *Co-ge-we-a* is representative of an important tradition in ethnic literature in which the relationship of author to audience, and the transmission of the author's work to the audience, is mediated by a midwife figure. ⟨. . .⟩

⟨But⟩ such annotation or translation is more often than not inaccurate ⟨. . . .⟩ Cogewea, for instance, is particularly offended by a white-authored novel called *The Brand*, which purports to describe half-breed life. ⟨. . .⟩ What really excites Cogewea's contempt, however, is the novelist's misuse of Indian words. She remarks to Jim LaGrinder, her half-breed suitor, "'It contains a few tribal phrases, supposedly the names of birds and animals. These have been conferred on some of the characters, or pet saddle horses; which, if properly translated, would shock the public immeasurably'" (91–93).

In Cogewea's objection to the white author's wrongful translation, how-ever, lies the means by which the ethnic writer *can* both preserve the traditions of her culture and mediate with the white world; here lies one solution to the problem of ethnic female authorship; here lies, so to speak, the trick. Who provided the white author of *The Brand* with these dirty Indian words? In doing so, the author's Indian "informant" (as the Indian is commonly described in many of these texts) participates in authorship of the text, in effect writing a subtext to *The Brand*, a subtext that functions as an inside Indian joke and that does preserve Indian language and culture.

Jim LaGrinder explains to Cogewea that he had had some contact with the white lady who wrote *The Brand*, and offers another story that explains the workings of ethnic authorship:

> I was there when the boys was a stuffin' one poor woman. It was at
> the first buffalo roundup when lots of people come to see the sight. A
> bunch of us riders was together when this here lady come up and
> begins askin' questions 'bout the buffaloes; and Injun names of flyin',
> walkin', and swimmin' things and a lot of bunk. Well, you know how
> the boys are. They sure locoed that there gal to a finish; and while
> she was a dashin' the information down in her little tablet, we was a
> thinkin' up more lies to tell her. We didn't savey she was writin' a real
> book, or maybe we would a been more careful. Yes, *maybe!* Why,
> them there writin' folks is dead easy pickin' for the cowpunchers.
> (93–94, Mourning Dove's emphasis)

If this strategy is available to the Indian, a good deal of his or her power is pre-served. The constant comments in *Co-ge-we-a* on strategies very like this one, indeed on authenticity itself, argue that the authenticity of the finished text is in fact compromised by McWhorter's "authorship," and that there exists a sub-text within the novel that is wholly Mourning Dove's. In a world in which whites are perceived as, and reveal themselves to be, treacherous authors, one must lie to them, and in lying, after all, one authors fictions.

In this light, incidents within the novel, such as the cowboys' farcical sendups of effete Easterners, can be interpreted as expressions of the insider's possession of authenticity. Only the insider knows the language, and language is an important weapon. This can be briefly illustrated by the example of Alfred Densmore, lured to the West by Western novels, disillusioned by the reality behind the romantic rhetoric: he expresses "vexation and disgust for the writers who had beguiled him to the 'wild and woolly'" (44). As Jim LaGrinder says, "'Well, you know how the boys are.'" They cannot resist playing on Densmore's ignorance of right language and bet him that he cannot ride a bronc. Densmore goes along, thinking that "bronc" is "a western phrase for donkey" (49), and promptly gets thrown by a very real unbroken horse. Knowledge of authentic language is a prerequisite for survival in a West that is "wild and woolly" in quite another way than Densmore understands.

If concerns about authenticity and explanations of inside texts so abound in the text, we might expect that Mourning Dove would indulge in some joking of her own. And, in fact, the text is riddled with tricks, some of which are, quite suitably, forever inaccessible to outsiders not well-versed in Okanogan culture, and which I can only guess at. Others are more easy to locate. Mourning Dove's hand is evident, for example, in the use of epigrams and chapter titles, some of which militate rather violently against the contents of the chapters. This is particularly true of chapters given over to the oral legends provided by the Stemteemä—which are, after all, close to authentic texts. The Stemteemä's story of the disastrous coming of the white man is related in a chapter titled "The Superior Race." The epigram is from Scott's "Lay of the Last Minstrel"; of course in this chapter the Stemteemä, or Mourning Dove herself, is the "last minstrel" singing a "lay" of a supposedly vanishing race. Longfellow's romanticized and inauthentic *Hiawatha* is similarly subverted. While in *Hiawatha* the male Nawadoha relates legends and visions, in *Co-ge-we-a* this is the Stemteemä's province. In affixing—or allowing McWhorter to do so—Longfellow's lines about Hiawatha's courtship to a chapter that describes the story of Green Blanket Feet, an Indian woman who married a white man with tragic consequences, or in affixing lines from "The Giaour" to a chapter in which the treacherous Densmore courts Cogewea, Mourning Dove turns a trick, inserts her own voice into McWhorter's didactic narrative, and creates an alternative text available to the insider. Indirectly, she claims authorship.

—Mary V. Dearborn, *Pocahontas's Daughters: Gender and Ethnicity in American Culture* (New York: Oxford University Press, 1986), 22–26

ALANNA KATHLEEN BROWN

To see ⟨. . .⟩ clearly Mourning Dove's understanding of the oral traditions she worked into the novel ⟨one should⟩ look at a story Mourning Dove transcribed about her great-grandmother, Pah-tah-heet-sa, a full blooded Nicola Indian woman ⟨. . . ,⟩ including the lengthy explanatory footnotes for McWhorter ⟨*Cogewea*, 1981, 24–25, 269⟩. ⟨. . .⟩

The contrast between Mourning Dove's story and the footnotes she feels compelled to write for McWhorter's benefit are very revealing. McWhorter is concerned with verifiable facts. Mourning Dove, on the other hand, receives the tale of her great-grandmother as a distillation of that woman's spirit, her essence, and because that story is also about an ancestor, it honors Mourning

Dove and her line. It is a family story and it has importance for the generations that will follow. The story is specific about some aspects of daily life such as the camas stick, and undoubtedly it denotes a particular place in the upper Columbia basin as one crosses the Canadian/United States border, but specific time and detailed description are wholly unnecessary to its function as a family story. They would be, it could be argued, disruptive. This is a narrative for a storyteller, easily animated in voice and gesture. But in English and on the printed page it is removed from the expressiveness of its own language and the power of immediate performance.

Much of Mourning Dove's narrative in *Cogewea, the Half-Blood* has this same storyteller immediacy. It is not difficult to see how the tales of the buckskin breeches or the grandmother yelling to the men on the thin ice could easily be transformed again into the realms of oral presentation. McWhorter's voice in the novel is quite different. He was, first and foremost, the amateur ethnographer, although his most memorable passages are the zealous diatribes against the corruption of United States government officials and Christian hypocrites. McWhorter was the teacher, the preacher, and the judge, when he inserted himself into the novel. Mourning Dove, by contrast, always remains the Indian storyteller.

Nowhere can this be better illustrated than in Stemteema's narratives. Stemteema's very mode of presentation belongs to a long tradition of oral presentation. Implicit in that tradition is the lived experience of the teller. When Stemteema announced that, "The story I am telling is true and I want you to keep it after I am gone. *Green Blanket Feet* was my best friend and she told me this tale after she came back to our tribe from the Blackfeet" (p. 165), Euro-American audiences tend to assume that this is only a story telling device, a frame to create authenticity. But for those within the oral tradition it is important to know who first told the tale or how the present speaker has been given the authority to recount it. The focus on the movement of the central character, the revelation of the message through Green-Blanket Feet's own painful journey, are all meant to create the simple, direct power of a parable.

At the core of Mourning Dove's stories there is always the human truth of lived experience. In a letter dated April 28, 1916, Mourning Dove remarks, "Green Blanket Feets granddaughter Susie Winegard is at the present living in Spokane. She saw my picture in the paper and hunted me up" ⟨24–26, 366⟩. Moreover, in a May 14, 1916 letter, Mourning Dove cautions McWhorter not to give so much personal history in a footnote on Green-Blanket Feet as to embarrass family members, "for she was a noted character, among the Colvilles" ⟨27–29, 366⟩. There is a sensitivity possessed by those nurtured in the oral tradition that Euro-Americans can miss entirely.

—Alanna Kathleen Brown, "Mourning Dove's Voice in *Cogewea*," *Wicazo Sa Review* 4, no. 2 (Fall 1988): 7–10

ALANNA KATHLEEN BROWN

In this second round of collaboration ⟨for what would become *Coyote Stories*⟩ a new tone was set. The letters show McWhorter becoming more technical about linguistic issues. He is paying attention to the Salish language for he wants the work to be creditable among scholars. He had become more aware of a world of experts with authority to judge their work. He also was troubled by language impurities that were creeping into the legends through translation and because of the Indian interactions with French and English speaking peoples. McWhorter wanted the tales to be as traditional as possible:

> In the legend: "The Great Spirit Names the Animal-people" there occurs this phrase, this sentence: En-pa-pah: (my papa) It is where Coyote's starving children accosted him when he entered the doorway of his tepee the evening before the naming of every one by the Great Spirit. You will recall it. Here is what I want:
> It appears to me that "papa" is too modern a word in this case. Did the Indians use the term "papa?" Could not the word be changed to convey a name more in keeping with the true Indian vocabulary? How would "parent" or "father" do? You are the one to determine the true way. I only thought that "papa" perhaps is not the best word in the premises. I want you to get these legends in the very best shape possible. Did the Indians have a word for "sire?" You fix it. I have already written you relative to "monkey". ⟨. . .⟩ (c. late 1921)

These inquiries became typical of their correspondence. Mourning Dove not only came to think in terms of syllables and accents when considering her own language, she struggled with the difficulty of spelling words in an alphabet that does not have Salish sounds. Moreover, the meanings of some Indian words had changed over time, or she could not get at the original meaning of a word because a tribe had died out.

> Spikst: is the word for "glove" in Okanagan, and I hardly think that the Indians used the fingered gloves in the early day, when they had no means of cutting them easily like we have in the present day. And a hand cover is hardly a word that would find correct meaning in the Indian language. So use speekist, with English diff. . . . . will be all O.K.
> Unless you want hand cover. I will try and write word. hard word to write[.] (c. late 1921)

There was even the further complication of multiple Indian languages and dialects. McWhorter asked: "In the Semteema's [sic] stories, and in these legends, the term 'sun-down' is used in the sense of one 'day' or 'days.' Is this the way you want it? I like it, as different from the 'sun' of the Yakimas and others. Tell me if O.K." Mourning Dove responded on the same sheet of paper:

> In answer to this, you can use your own judgment. They are both correct in the Okanogan dialect. It seems that each is used, according to the speakers idea of speech. Usually the Indians call a day "light day" and night "dark night." According to what they are speaking off. And sun-down is used as well as sun, by one Indians that live in different locations on the Reservation. This Reserve have quite a few varied dialects, similar to one another, and yet not the same. There are Lakes. Colville. Lower and northren Okanogans. Wenatchees. Nes Perce. San Poils. Ketle River Indians. (c. late 1922)

McWhorter's curiosity was insatiable. He hungered to understand distinctions that were not clear to him, and Mourning Dove became, at times, McWhorter's teacher. In a long letter dated November 22, 1921, she explains that there is a difference between Coyote's *squ-tenk* power and the *shoó-mesh* of the other animals. A year later McWhorter was still asking questions. Why does grizzly-bear throw off his summer-coat and "don his shaggiest winter-coat" while "flashing his new, sharp summer teeth" (c. late 1922). Mourning Dove explains:

> Summer teeth seems to be correct as far as Indian dilect is concerned in speech. It is supposed to be in legends that after a bear's winters rest he comes out with sharper teeth then in the fall, when he had used the teeth all summer. So naturally winter teeth would not be as sharp, not as sharp as summer teeth. You might change that, and put summer teeth with his summer coat. But it seems that the story teller wants to impress the idea that Grizzle bear wanted to be seen in his fiercest look. So it speaks of its shaggy winter coat, and summer new sharp teeth. You might make a note on this effect, and explain why it speaks thus. (c. late 1922)

Theirs had become a genuine dialogue. Mourning Dove and McWhorter spoke directly to one another. Their material was known by them both. They had created a common language and common goals. McWhorter did not move, as he had done with *Cogewea*, from editor into co-writer. The manuscript for Okanogan Sweat House includes 38 stories and is clearly Mourning Dove's work, with grammatical editing and notes by McWhorter, and Indian names and spellings which McWhorter and Mourning Dove agreed upon.

—Alanna Kathleen Brown, "The Evolution of Mourning Dove's *Coyote Stories*," *Studies in American Indian Literatures* 4, nos. 1 and 2 (Summer/Fall 1992): 170–72

PETER G. BEIDLER

⟨In denouncing the racist elements of *The Brand* in chapter 10,⟩ Cogewea overemphasizes those elements and reacts to them out of proportion to their importance in the novel. And her reaction tells us more about her own feelings than it does about *The Brand*. ⟨. . .⟩

⟨. . .T⟩he real reason for Cogewea's angry rejection of *The Brand* has little to do with the book itself or with the critical principle of literary racism. It has to do, rather, with Cogewea's own sensitivity about being a half-blood and her hopes for escaping her Indianness through a white education and a white marriage. If I am right, Cogewea is less a reliable literary critic than a character who uses literary criticism to disguise her dissatisfaction with being a half-blood.

Of course, there are reasons for skepticism about my view of Cogewea's reading of *The Brand*. Are we really to believe that readers of Mourning Dove's novel would pick up these intertextual connections between *The Brand* and *Cogewea*? Perhaps not, but why else is *The Brand* mentioned by name in chapter 10, and why else is so much made of Cogewea's impassioned reaction to it? Are we really to believe that Cogewea misreads *The Brand* in a way consistent with her confused feelings about the inferiority of Indians? Perhaps not, but why else does she get so angry at so silly a novel, and why else is she so eager to marry a man who has nothing to recommend him except that he is white? Are we really to believe that Cogewea identifies with what she sees as anti-maternal feelings in a male character because she wants to deny her own Indian ancestry, her own Indian mother? Perhaps not, but why else would Mourning Dove have Cogewea come down so hard on Henry's supposed hatred of the mother he, in fact, loves and reverences? Are we really to believe that Cogewea criticizes *The Brand* for a largely imaginary racism? Perhaps not, but why else would Mourning Dove have Cogewea portray as racist a novel that, for all its Anglocentrism, is less racist than she makes it sound, and why else would Mourning Dove have Cogewea try to conceal from herself the assimilationist tendencies in her own troubled heart?

My view of Cogewea's misreading of *The Brand* is corroborated by her reaction to another story later in *Cogewea*: Stemteemä's story of her friend Green-blanket Feet in chapter 19. That story, one of the most memorable narrative units in the novel, has a clear message for Cogewea. It is a message, however, that she does not want to hear, a message similar to what she found in *The Brand*: that young Indian women cannot trust handsome, slick, white easterners. Green-blanket Feet, we recall, married a white man in an Indian ceremony and had two children by him. After several years, he left to go home to his white wife, taking the children with him. Green-blanket Feet followed but was cruelly mistreated by her white husband. On the journey, she tried to steal her children back and take them home with her, but he caught and beat her. Finally, in desperation, she stole away one of the children at night and tried to return to her people, but the child died on the journey home. Green-blanket Feet tells the story to Stemteemä, closing with this warning: "'Let the maidens of my tribe shun the Shoyahpee [white man]. His words are poison! his touch is death'" (Cogewea, 176). Not quite trusting Cogewea to get the point, Stemteemä specifically reinterprets the message to her granddaughter: "Cogewea; you must be more careful of that Shoyahpee [Densmore]. I do not like to have you with him so much. You must quit going with him alone. It is against the rules of our race for a maiden to do so. You must stop it! He only seeks to harm you. The fate of Green-blanket Feet is for you . . . unless you turn from him'" (Cogewea, 176).

Cogewea's reaction to the story is anger: "Cogewea's ivory teeth closed firm and her tapering fingers dug into the shaggy buffalo robe before she ventured self defense" (Cogewea, 176). She declares, "'The young bird flies more sprightly than do the old. The Shoyahpee girls go out with their men friends and nobody cares'" (Cogewea, 177–78). Wanting to be like the white girls and "fly more sprightly" than the old-style Indians, Cogewea rejects her grandmother's warning. Stemteemä cruelly reminds Cogewea that "'she is not full Shoyahpee. She is only half! She must forget her white blood and follow after her Okanogan ancestors'" (Cogewea, 177). Cogewea makes no oral response to that statement, but "she rebelled at the thought that she must not love the fair skinned Easterner too well" (Cogewea, 177). In rejecting the story of Green-blanket Feet, Cogewea repeats the response she had earlier had to The Brand. It is very much in character for Cogewea, when she does not like the message, to reject both the storyteller and the story that convey the message. We should recall that her own life had involved a story whose warning she had also ignored. Her white father, like Green-blanket Feet's husband, had used and then abandoned his Indian wife. Cogewea denies the relevance of such stories to her own situation until it is almost too late. At the end of the novel, however, she comes to see the relevance of all these stories to her own life, and she marries the half-blood Jim.

—Peter G. Beidler, "Literary Criticism in Cogewea: Mourning Dove's Protagonist Reads The Brand," American Indian Culture and Research Journal 19, no. 2 (1995): 56, 60–62

SUSAN K. BERNARDIN

The multivalent title—Cogewea, The Half-Blood: A Depiction of the Great Montana Cattle Range—acts as an index to the entangled issues addressed in the novel. "Cogewea," Okanogan for chipmunk, suggests native authenticity, but "half-blood"—a sign of miscegenation and hybrid identity—questions it. The final part of the title evokes the elegiac mode of conventional westerns, foreshadowing the issue of mixed genres within the text. Like its disjunctive title, the novel's confusing array of "voices," usually attributed to its mixed-authorship and often read as a fundamental problem, leads us to Mourning Dove's elusive and shifting narrative authority. McWhorter's revisions, intended to bolster the text's authority by counteracting Mourning Dove's use of vernacular, indirectly promote the novel's thematic focus on the protagonist's liminality. Thus Cogewea's abruptly shifting voice—from ranch vernacular to Chinook and Salish terms to formal English—embodies the kinds of cultural and linguistic dislocations experienced by Native Americans in the early twentieth century. In this and other ways, *Cogewea* manages to exceed the bounds intended by either Mourning Dove or McWhorter.

Similarly, surveying the evidence of their mixed authorship in the text reveals the mixed genres through whose adaptations and reformulations we can hear Mourning Dove's voice. Undermining McWhorter's conception of *Cogewea* as an ethnographic, historical document is a trickster subtext that contests all master narratives about Indians. This ironic mode, so unlike McWhorter's editorial inscriptions, emerges in a range of narrative and generic strategies which display a highly self-conscious deployment of familiar tropes and formulaic plots. McWhorter's professed lack of familiarity with romance forms and his contempt for westerns perhaps prevented him from detecting the skillful generic adaptations that characterize the novel. Mourning Dove's selective disruption of expectations encoded in gender-marked romance and western forms enables the text's revision of the vanishing, victimized Indian and demonized "half-blood" embedded in popular cultural and official memory. Specifically, Mourning Dove strategically appropriates popular forms in order to produce a hybrid text designed to "bear the burden" of mixed-blood experience ⟨Bill Ashcroft et al., *The Empire Writes Back*, 1989, 38⟩.

Among those popular forms, *Cogewea* aligns itself with a tradition of Euro-American women's fiction whose different versions address the struggles of a young woman, orphaned or otherwise unprotected, who must negotiate economic and sexual dangers in order to emerge married by narrative's end. By self-consciously adopting elements of the sentimental romance plot popularized by nineteenth-century Anglo-American women's fiction, Mourning Dove gained access to a narrative form that enabled her to address the culturally taboo issue of miscegenation. ⟨. . .⟩

By inscribing sentimental conventions within a mixed-blood woman's story, *Cogewea* draws attention to the linguistic, social, and geographic liminality produced by mixed ancestry and Anglo education. Similarly, the text reinvents another popular form, the western, by wrenching it from its Euro-American foundations. *Cogewea* incorporates familiar trademarks of the popular western—ranch humor, stock figures, open expanses, a silent cowboy hero—but repeatedly ironizes them.

—Susan K. Bernardin, "Mixed Messages: Authority and Authorship in Mourning Dove's *Cogewea, The Half-Blood: A Depiction of the Great Montana Cattle Range,*" *American Literature* 67, no. 3 (September 1995): 495–97

LINDA K. KARELL

It is important to remember that Mourning Dove had completed a first draft of *Cogewea* before meeting McWhorter in 1914. Although we no longer have access to this draft, we know that it was a novel-length fictional Western Romance, a localized variation on a traditional European literary genre. Moreover, as we consider the implications of Mourning Dove's and McWhorter's collaboration, it is important to resist constructing her absent first draft as a destroyed example of "authentic" Native American literature to avoid simplifying an enormously complex relationship into that of a victimizer and victim. Relations between race and gender (a Native American woman and a white male editor) are at the heart of this collaborative effort. Citing a 1924 letter from McWhorter to Joseph Latimer in which he claims "I feel that the publication of this work, coming as it does from the pen of an Indian, would be a potent factor in bringing about a reformation and cleaning up of the Indian Department," Alanna Kathleen Brown ⟨"Legacy Profile: Mourning Dove," 1989, 54⟩ has written that,

> The novel now had two writers with separate purposes. Mourning Dove's story remained focused on the spiritual struggles of her generation and the blatant racism of the times. McWhorter's sections added extensive ethnographic commentary to the novel to preserve a knowledge of Native American ways he believed were quickly vanishing. He also used the work to attack the Christian hypocrisy of his peers and the corruption of federal agents. The disruption to the narrative was severe.

Even without the original draft to compare with the published version of *Cogewea*, Brown's assessment of narrative disruption is undeniable. Dexter Fisher ⟨in *Cogewea*, 1981, xiv⟩ remarks that the novel "sags at times under the weight of vituperation," and Paula Gunn Allen ⟨*The Sacred Hoop*, 1992, 83⟩ has referred to *Cogewea* as "a maimed—I should say martyred—book." In varying degrees, each of these assessments emphasizes what appear to be the negative effects of the narrative disruptions and implicitly regrets that the novel is not, at the very least, a more unified collaboration. I understand the text as one marked by splinters and fractures, as resisting simplistic and stereotyped understandings of an essentialized Native American harmony, one perhaps desired by a white audience in search of a redemptive spirituality. Rather than being a failure because it does not achieve a wholeness, *Cogewea*'s accomplishment is that it refuses such narrow expectations. The novel questions the very possibility of such wholeness. Mourning Dove presents us with the complexities of the bicultural identity she claimed, but she did not attempt to claim for herself a position transcending the confusion represented by such an unstable and culturally unrecognized identity. She did not position herself "outside" of her culture—which was, by the time she wrote, already a mixture of Native and white beliefs.

I do not mean to suggest that it is unimportant either that Mourning Dove's original text was revised by McWhorter without her full knowledge of the extent of his changes, or that the voices in the text we currently have are impossible to definitely ascribe to either author. On the contrary, to dismiss the implications of that violation and that uncertainty is to employ theoretical insights in order to enact yet another self-interested violence on the text. But from its title page to its conclusion, *Cogewea* insists on the collaborative and performative nature of literature, whether oral or written, and makes the particular Western desire to locate a single author who (himself) writes an individual text by dint of artistic brilliance seem obtusely wrongheaded, a yearning born of anxiety and doubt.

In a very literal way, neither Mourning Dove nor McWhorter could have produced *Cogewea* without the other. And at the same time, this particular collaboration is not "the same as" the collaboration, across seasons and generations, that produces Native American oral literature. In other words, collaboration itself is a contested term and is neither inherently benign nor politically neutral. With *Cogewea* we can see a particular cultural struggle, one which the text performs with each reading. This collaborative effort reveals a more complex story—and one ultimately more spiritually challenging and historically informative—than reading it for harmony would generate.

—Linda K. Karell, "'This Story I Am Telling You Is True': Collaboration and Literary Authority in Mourning Dove's *Cogewea*," *The American Indian Quarterly* 19, no. 4 (Fall 1995): 458–59

MARTHA L. VIEHMANN

Lucullus McWhorter ⟨. . .⟩ appended notes to the novel that explain Native words, verify historical references, and expand on injustice as a theme. The information establishes the authentic grounding of the book in Native American experience. The emphasis on authenticity gives us a context for the book, but it does not help readers grasp the literary workings of it. McWhorter's notes to the *stemteemä's* story of Green-blanket Feet provide a good example. This is one of three tales that the grandmother relates; all of them are central to the novel, for they deal with European–Native contact and provide a mythic model for the fictional plot. By including the legend, Mourning Dove reworks the popular romance through the addition of folklore, and her use of the *stemteemä's* voice contributes to the dialogism of the text. McWhorter's treatment of the legend in his footnotes represents the collaborative aspect of mixed descent and demonstrates his own tendency toward a historical point of view. ⟨. . .⟩

The chapter in which the tale of Green-blanket Feet is related rates more notes than any other. Most of them define Okanogan words or describe Native customs and clarify events in the story. Note four is particularly helpful, for it describes the significance of Green-blanket Feet's acts when she escapes from the Blackfeet. McWhorter tells us that by touching the chief's sacred objects and mimicking their ritual use, she desecrates them, destroying their magic and humiliating the chief (293–4). McWhorter's remarks help give meaning to an otherwise mysterious action. Notes such as this show the benefits of the collaboration and the strength arising from the "mixed heritage" of the book.

However, the first note to the story of Green-blanket Feet is especially curious. Mourning Dove describes a suspenseful scene in which Green-blanket Feet plunges into a large badger hole to escape from her armed husband. McWhorter appends a note asserting that such large holes "are often met with in the loose desert soil" (293). Here and throughout the book, McWhorter reveals his anxiety that Mourning Dove's words be taken as true and shows his lack of faith in the power of stories. The note interrupts the scene, distracting the reader with facts. Instead of seeing Green-blanket Feet cowering in a hole, we see McWhorter hovering about the text like a nervous hen, trying to assure us that the words are true.

McWhorter's concern for veracity and detail also comes across in the last, lengthy footnote to the chapter. He begins by saying that "in the Stemteemä's narrative of *Green-blanket Feet*, the author has purposely incorporated incidents connected with two or three different occurrences" (295). McWhorter then repeats the story as passed down through Green-blanket Feet's children. His tale can be as compelling as Mourning Dove's version, but his main concern seems to be factual accuracy, with names, places, and dates listed. He concludes with a few paragraphs about the fickleness of the Indian Bureau in dealing with children of mixed parentage. This information is not pertinent to the story of Green-blanket Feet or to Mourning Dove's reasons for relating it. Instead, it contributes to the arguments against the Indian Bureau and to the development of the broader theme of institutionally based injustice meted out to Native Americans, primary concerns of McWhorter. When McWhorter tells us that the author purposely connects several distinct occurrences, it is not clear whether he simply wants to set the story straight or if he truly appreciates Mourning Dove's artistry. By blending several tales of woe, Mourning Dove intensifies the pathos, building up to Green-blanket Feet's declaration of the Great Spirit's displeasure and her final warning to all Okanogan women to "shun the Shoyahpee. His words are poison! his touch is death." If the protagonist of the inserted tale has not made the point clear, the *stemteemä* repeats it, telling Cogewea that "the fate of Green-blanket Feet is for you; my grandchild unless you turn from him" (176). Where Mourning Dove relies on a character and narrator from a story within the story to express her theme, McWhorter adds an accumulation of facts to sway the readers.

—Martha L. Viehmann, "'My People . . . My Kind': Mourning Dove's *Cogewea, the Half-Blood* As a Narrative of Mixed Descent," in *Early Native American Writing: New Critical Essays,* ed. Helen Jaskoski (New York: Cambridge University Press, 1996), 214–16

B I B L I O G R A P H Y

Cogewea, the Half-Blood: A Depiction of the Great Montana Cattle Range. 1927.
Coyote Stories. 1933.
Tales of the Okanogans. 1976.
Mourning Dove: A Salishan Autobiography. 1990.
Mourning Dove's Stories. 1991.

WENDY ROSE

B. 1948

WENDY ROSE was born in Oakland, California, in 1948. Like many Native American writers, she is of mixed blood: her father is Hopi, and her mother is a descendant of an almost extinct tribe, the Miwoks. Wendy grew up not on a reservation but in a city—San Francisco. This may be one of the reasons that her poetry is among the only work by contemporary Native American writers to confront directly the situation of the urbanized Indian, although Rose says that while she was growing up she thought that if she lived on a reservation, her life would be much simpler—that "everything would come together."

Dropping out of high school in the 1960s, Rose began writing poetry, which she published in early anthologies of Native American writing under the pseudonym Chiron Khanshendel. Later, at the University of California at Berkeley, she earned a degree in anthropology—one of few Native Americans to do so—and has compiled a bibliography of Native American writing that spans over 200 years. She studied archaeology as well, which has been useful in work she has done with the American Indian Movement to protect traditional burial grounds.

In addition to her writing and scholarly work, Rose is an accomplished painter; her line drawings often accompany the texts of Native American anthologies and critical editions. Learning to draw, paint, and write poetry, says Rose, were processes of self-healing for her, almost forms of therapy. She balances this statement by saying that in the non-Indian world, the arts provide solace for feeling isolated, which is very different from the Indian understanding of the arts.

Rose teaches at the University of California at Berkeley, but she has, only somewhat jokingly, referred to herself as a "spy" in the academic world. Married to a Japanese American, she says that she and her husband are always moving between cultures and that they never quite feel comfortable in either. She has referred to her "hybrid status" as a way to explain her sense of displacement between mainstream and Native American cultures; but this same hybrid status is in part what fuels her poetry and paintings. Rose gives eloquent voice to those engaged in the difficult act of balancing between cultures.

CRITICAL EXTRACTS

ANDREW WIGET

Bones are ubiquitous in Rose's poetry because they provide a metonymic locus for relationships to place and time that can then be caught up in a larger, coherent imagery of Body, both body as resource and body as residuum. Each aspect of body imagery complements the other. As a resource, it is visceral knowledge, felt pain or pleasure that motivates her poetry. "I began as a song or an agony, / a buzz from the mother of tongues." "These words must be remembered / as butchered things, as bits of life / thrown down" (*Lost Copper* 69). As residuum, the fear of death is expressed as a fear that the poetic self, having become the self-consuming artifact, will exhaust itself or be annihilated by masks that smother its uniqueness and vitality:

> death came carried by words
> in weakening meter, in the false welcome
> of parentheses, in the open mouth
> of another dead poet's anthology. (*Lost Copper* 62)

The urgency of purpose with which this understanding of art endows Rose's writing is responsible in no small part, I think, for her great attention to her craft. Her poetic skills are evident on every page and are one of the greatest sources of pleasure in her work. Look, for instance, at how she accelerates the rhythm of "Potsherds" (*Lost Copper* 58). Note how the first period doesn't come until the end of four long, quiet lines: then come eight shorter lines, five of which have strong punctuation breaks to quicken them further; then comes the final solitary thirteenth line, which skates off on sibilance into infinity. Rose also has an excellent ear for sound. She can subtly modulate between back-vowel sounds: "You sang and murmured, water over stone, / a tumble of flute and drum and bamboo clacker" (*Lost Copper* 76).

Ironically, despite the vitality that the act of writing stimulates, because a poem is finally a made thing, a writer who identifies closely with the act of writing can feel that publication is a kind of death, a final chilling into print, the displacement from the made to the maker. In "The Poet as Unclaimed Corpse" she traces the life of the poet and poem:

> I began as a song or an agony
> a buzz from the mother of tongues,
> I end like that, laid out in diagrams,
> to be buried in a strange land. (*Lost Copper* 62)

I suspect that the continual revision that marks Rose's poems when they reap-
pear in subsequent volumes is an attempt to reaffirm the poetic self in a strategy of continual remaking that defeats the closure of print.
    —Andrew Wiget, "Blue Stones, Bones, and Troubled Silver: The Poetic Craft of Wendy
    Rose" (1983), reprinted in *Studies in American Indian Literatures* 5, no. 2 (Summer 1993): 31–32

CAROL HUNTER

⟨Interview with Wendy Rose by Carol Hunter⟩

CH: You're a painter, as well as a writer. Much of your painting deals with
mythical characters. How much of the oral tradition, the stories and the
mythology of the Hopi tradition influenced your writing and your painting?

WR: Quite a bit, yet it's a kind of an ironic response at the same time. They
have influenced my painting a great deal because the images are so strong and
they touch something in me so deeply that the only response is to paint it, to
express it as a visual image. When I'm painting these figures, I'm painting my
own response to them in a way. I am responding to something in the traditions, then letting it come into me and flow out, part tradition and part me,
onto the paper. But you know I've always had trouble listening to storytellers
or even listening to someone read fiction out loud because I get caught up in
some little detail, some individual image, and I can't let it go. The whole story
stops for me at that point and I have to express my response to that image. The
frame freezes for me and I have to deal with that frame. Meanwhile the story
has continued and come to a conclusion, and there I am way back toward the
beginning somewhere. Also I have not been exposed to oral traditions and this
has been a big gap in my upbringing. It's like growing up with bad eyesight
and being given glasses as an adult. You missed a lot and you're aware of it, and
this has something to do with how you interpret the new, sharp world around
you, but you can never go back and re-grow your life with good eyes. You can
see, finally, but your interpretation of what you see will always be influenced
by the years you didn't see clearly. It could be no other way and it doesn't
mean that you are wrong, or that you are misinterpreting what you see. It only
means you are seeing it differently than those who grew up with good vision.
Since I have bad eyes and didn't get glasses until I was about eight years old,
I feel pretty confident about the analogy. The lack of exposure to traditional
storytelling has been a big gap in my background and when I have encountered the storytelling, in my teens and as an adult, I have been aware that I am
in the presence of something big and important, something that has held people together when military defense couldn't. I envy those Indian writers who

were able to move smoothly and naturally from the oral tradition to the written. My tendency is to acknowledge that they are the *real* Indian writers while I am not; yet, when I think about it, I realize that many Indians are in my position so I, too, represent a part of Indian Country as it is now.
—Carol Hunter, "A MELUS Interview: Wendy Rose," *MELUS* 10, no. 3 (Fall 1983): 76–77

JOSEPH BRUCHAC

⟨Interview with Wendy Rose by Joseph Bruchac⟩

JB: In your poem "Builder Kachina," you have these lines—"a half breed goes from one-half home to the other." And of course *The Halfbreed Chronicles* is the name of the collection you just read that first poem from. That word "halfbreed" seems to be very important to you. What is it? What does that mean?

WR: Well, again, I have to answer on at least two different levels. One is the obvious thing of being biologically halfbreed, being of mixed race. I was in a situation where I was physically separated from one-half of my family and rejected by the half that brought me up. And in this case it was because of what there is in me that belonged to the other half. The way that a lot of us put it is you're too dark to be white and you're too white to be Indian. James Welch expressed it well in *The Death of Jim Loney* where Jim Loney answers someone who says to him (to paraphrase), "oh, you're so lucky that you can have the best of both worlds and choose whether or not at a given moment you will be Indian or you will be white." And he says, "it's not that we have the best of both worlds, it's that we don't really have anything of either one." I think that's really a very true statement. You don't get to pick and choose but rather you're in a position where you have no choice whatsoever. I was in that situation where the white part of my family had absolutely no use for any other races that came into the family. The white part of the family had no use for it. The Indian half is in a situation where, among the Hopi, the clan and your identity comes through the mother, and without the Hopi mother it doesn't matter if your father was fullblooded or not, you can't be Hopi. So that left me in that situation. The first years of writing, perhaps, the motivation from the very beginning was to try to come to terms with being in that impossible situation. But then maturing as a person, halfbreed takes on a different connotation and that's where *The Halfbreed Chronicles* are coming from. Now *The Halfbreed Chronicles* depict a number of people, and genetics doesn't have a great deal to do with it. For instance, the poem "Georgeline" is relating to people who are a fullblood Lakota family. There are other people who are depicted in *Halfbreed Chronicles* who would not be identified as halfbreed. People who are

Japanese-American. People who are Mexican-Indian but spent their lives as sideshow freaks. People like Robert Oppenheimer. You don't think of these people in the same sense as you usually think of halfbreeds. But my point is that, in an important way, the way that I grew up is symptomatic of something much larger than Indian-white relations. History and circumstances have made halfbreeds of all of us.

JB: Then maybe you wouldn't be offended by my bringing in something I just thought of . . . a quotation from Matthew Arnold. He described himself back in the Victorian era—"one half dead, the other powerless to be born." There seems to be, as you see it, a world dilemma not just of people of mixed Indian and white ancestry but of the modern culture that we find ourselves faced with.

WR: Yeah, and I think that the point does come out in *The Halfbreed Chronicles* because one of the responses that I get is from people who are genetically all Caucasian, or all black, or all Indian; people who are genetically not of mixed race come up to me afterwards and say I know just what you mean by those poems. I feel like a halfbreed, too. So I know the message is getting through.
    —Joseph Bruchac, "The Bones Are Alive," in *Survival This Way* (Tucson: University of Arizona Press, 1987), 254–56

ROBERT L. BERNER

Her eighth book ⟨*Going to War with All My Relations*⟩, balancing characteristic earlier poems and recent uncollected work, is a valuable survey of her poetic career and an indication of her present concerns. ⟨. . .⟩

    Much of Rose's energy originates in painful memory of her mixed origins (Indian, German, English, Scottish). Her father gave her a Hopi identity which was only racial, and her fate—to discover Hopi culture only by an act of will and professional study—is reflected in the last line of an early poem about her father: "I grow but do not live." In spite of this, her mixed ancestry has always been a source of her strength and wisdom. A recent poem, significantly titled "If I Am Too Brown or Too White for You," makes clear her recognition that her impulse to poetry derives from that complex ancestry, and her beautiful tribute to a German pioneer great-great-grandmother ends with her recognition that German and American Indian historical experiences, though not simultaneous, are parallel: "Do you remember the tribes / that so loved their land / before the roll / of Roman wheels?"

    These poems seem more effective, both as art and as moral statement, than those which are more consciously and explicitly "social." "Yellow

Ribbons, Baghdad 1991," for example, is an attempt—unsuccessful in my view—to equate Iraqi civilians killed in the Gulf War with the victims of the Sand Creek massacre. Much more successful and certainly more moving are those poems which derive from the concerns expressed in her explanation in her preface of the terms of the book's title. The "war" is our common struggle to maintain our "relations" to one another, to all living things, and to the maternal earth. The maternal principle appears again and again in the poems and is implicit in "To the Vision Seekers, Remember This," in which scientists are asked to remember that all science derives from the earth itself: "it is women, / all women, where you come from, / Earth the one to remember."

—Robert L. Berner, [Review of *Going to War with All My Relations*], *World Literature Today* 68, no. 2 (Spring 1994): 408–9

ENID DAME

Poems that deal directly with ⟨. . .⟩ the ways a dominant culture turns a conquered one into artifact ⟨. . .⟩ appear throughout Rose's career. Cumulatively read ⟨in *Bone Dance*⟩, their effect is stunning. In the early (1976) "Long Division: a Tribal History," the Native people "are bought and divided/into clay pots." In the powerful "I Expected My Skin and My Blood to Ripen," the speaker is a Native woman killed at Wounded Knee, her "leggings taken like in a rape" and sold for $275. "Three Thousand Dollar Death Song" is an angry response to an invoice for "Nineteen American Indian skeletons" received casually at a museum. "For the White Poets Who Would be Indians" castigates the "temporary tourism" of such poets, who mistake face paint and ritualistic motions for authentic cultural experience. "Retrieving Osceola's Head" tells of a Seminole chief's head removed by a white doctor and used as a device to frighten/punish children. "Notes on a Conspiracy" suggests a reason for this ghoulish cycle of annihilation/preservation: "They blame us for their guilt." What this cycle extends to other cultures is demonstrated in "Truganinny," in which a Tasmanian woman correctly fears that her body will be used as a museum exhibit after her death.

Perhaps the strongest and most moving poem in this volume is "Julia," a dramatic monologue spoken by Julia Pastrana, a Mexican Indian circus performer, dubbed "Lion Lady" because of her excessive body hair. She marries her white manager, who she believes loves her. After she dies, her husband has both Julia and their dead son (who shared her physical condition) stuffed, mounted, and displayed—for monetary gain. The shocking cruelty of this act—a perfect metaphor for cultural appropriation—is contrasted with Julia's delicate, wistful voice:

O tell me again how you admire my hands how my jasmine tea is rich and strong my singing sweet, my eyes so dark you would lose yourself swimming.

—Enid Dame, [Review of Bone Dance: New and Selected Poems, 1965–1993], Belles Lettres: A Review of Books by Women 10, no. 1 (Fall 1994): 87

DARRYL BABE WILSON

Bone Dance leads us on a meandering path across the land and into the lives of distant native nations, north, south, east. It causes our spirits to follow—to the museum, to the grave, to the mountains and the rivers, to Santa Barbara Mission and its walls filled with native skeletons. In Bone Dance, Rose leads us to enter Loo Wit ("Mount St. Helens, Washington State"), feeling her pain of assault, witnessing her anger, and surveying her spiritual explosion caused by rape:

She was sleeping
but she heard
the boot scrape,
the creaking floor,
felt the pull of the blanket
from her thin shoulder (p. 52).

Rose states that she sometimes feels like Julia Pastrana, "The World's Ugliest Woman" ("Julia," p. 60), and I wonder how this can be. There is such ferocity in her presentation, such intensity in her meaning. There is the continuous and beautiful march directly toward oppression, led by the wisdom, "We have learned to barricade the village and have our weapons close at hand" (p. 83). There is no room, no time to be "ugliest," only time for exposing the crimes of a society that entered this hemisphere with malice aforethought, a malice that grows in intensity even as it fears its own extinction.

Rose gives us a unique anthropological view into the peculiar curiosity that leads or beckons the scientific mind as it searches the resting places of the natural beings of this continent in a drive to continue its degradation of all our relations. She states that she is identified as a "protest poet." Perhaps. That is shallow. She speaks with the eloquence of a worried mother. Protest, no. Truth, painful truth, yes.

Rose opens Bone Dance acknowledging her people and closes it with a caution about Coyote. Somehow Coyote has taken the gatchue-mo (exact image) of the scientists that surround her as she labors in the field and in the earth. But there is so much more to her spirit than an anthropologist or a poet. In

Yellow Ribbons (p. 88) she captures the power of the spirit that must not surrender,

> At least we fought, the patriarch said
> heaving the last of his home on his back.
> At least we did not die like victims
> sucking poison into our lungs
> but like warriors of God.

It is difficult to summarize the power of the thought that emanates from this work. It is a special combination of the study of anthropology guided by the ancient wisdom of two great nations, the Miwok of California and the Hopi of Arizona. But if it is necessary to simmer its contents until only a syrup is left in the bottom of the pail, there will be two words written there by a finger of knowledge: *unique* and *powerful*.

—Darryl Babe Wilson, [Review of *Bone Dance: New and Selected Poems, 1965–1993*], *American Indian Culture and Research Journal* 18, no. 3 (1994): 277–78

B I B L I O G R A P H Y

Hopi Roadrunner Dancing. 1974.
Long Division: A Tribal History. 1976, 1981.
Academic Squaw: Reports to the World from the Ivory Tower. 1977.
Aboriginal Tattooing in California. 1979.
Builder Kachina: A Home-Going Cycle. 1979.
Lost Copper. 1980.
What Happened When the Hopi Hit New York. 1982.
The Halfbreed Chronicles and Other Poems. 1985.
Going to War with All My Relations. 1993.
Bone Dance: New and Selected Poems, 1965–1993. 1994.
Now Poof, She Is Gone. 1994.

LESLIE MARMON SILKO

B. 1948

LESLIE MARMON SILKO is of mixed ancestry—Mexican, Laguna Pueblo, and white. She originally intended to be a lawyer in order to fight the injustices perpetrated against Native peoples; to that end, she attended several semesters of law school at the University of New Mexico. That career path ended, however, when she took a creative writing class and realized that the writing she had been doing all her life without thinking much about it could actually become a career—and combat injustice at the same time. Silko's activist politics would never be far below the surface of her poetry and novels.

Both Silko's celebrated first novel, *Ceremony* (1977), and her most recent novel, *Almanac of the Dead* (1991), were written, she says, to counterbalance historical inaccuracies about Native peoples. Both books reflect her radical politics not only in content, but also in form, combining past and present, poetry and prose, English and Laguna languages. *Ceremony* is a novel that incorporates the traditions, poetry, and stories of the Laguna Pueblo and Navajo tribes with the harsh realities of America after the Korean war; Silko describes *Almanac* as a "763-page indictment for five hundred years of theft, murder, pillage, and rape."

The central character of *Ceremony*, for which Silko is best known, is a young man named Tayo, an emotionally and psychically wounded veteran of the Korean War; the novel charts his healing process, which is enabled by a Navajo priest named Betonie. The male characters in this novel should not detract from her feminism, Silko says; the Laguna people do not in fact have the concept of "feminism," she has explained, because they have such a strong tradition of equal treatment between the sexes. Silko gives fictional tribute to feminine power through a character who appears in many of her stories: Yellow Woman, which is also the name given to Pueblo girls during ritual ceremonies.

Using a traditional name, and thus creating an allusion to a traditional ritual, is one of the ways Silko hopes to connect her work—and her readers—to the world around them. The theme of connection—lacking it and searching for it—pervades her work, but she says it is not unique to the writing of Native American writers. Instead, she says, this theme is something she finds in all contemporary fiction written by those who are from cultures that have been dismissed and diminished by mainstream American society. Making connections, she says, is crucial: without connection there is no way to remedy the situation of being seen as "Other."

Silko has been the recipient of many awards, including a MacArthur Foundation Fellowship and an NEA Discovery Grant.

CRITICAL EXTRACTS

REYES GARCÍA

There are many overtly political themes in *Ceremony* ⟨Signet, 1978⟩, in the commonly accepted notion of "political" which points toward atomistic conflicts of interest resolved at the "social" level by means of varying degrees of "government" intervention. Yet its clearest political themes revolve around the uranium mining which followed the first nuclear blast at White Sands, New Mexico, and around the loss and recovery of Indian lands—for example, lands taken from the native residents of Laguna Pueblo by loggers and ranchers who treat Tayo so badly in the novel (pp. 192–210).

Of course these themes are inseparable, since the uranium used for making nuclear weapons is mined mostly on Native American lands by large multinational corporations—Laguna lands being a primary source of it. The nuclear issue is inseparable from the politics of exterminism alluded to earlier.

This backgrounding begins to clarify the fundamental geographical conception of politics at work in the novel, a conception which emerges from the way land is understood. A major "plot" of Tayo's story lies in the integration of Tayo into Laguna Pueblo society and in the acceptance of Tayo's story into its history. *Ceremony* may be said to culminate down in the kiva, within the earthen chamber of the elders, where political life overtakes Tayo as he recounts his story to the medicine man Ku'oosh and the other old men who formally welcome Tayo home. In *Ceremony* the feeling of being at home and of belonging to the land realized by Tayo derives from a special sense of place that is also participation in culture and community.

Laguna poet and critic Paula Gunn Allen, speaking for all indigenous peoples, puts all this simply: "We are the land" ⟨"The Psychological Landscape of *Ceremony*," 1979, 7⟩. Tayo first begins to comprehend this truth through intimacies of the flesh as well as through the experience of ceremony. The dancer Nightswan introduces Tayo to his own body's connection to earth. She teaches him how to feel this connection as sensuous contour. At Nightswan's, even indoors, the room "pulsed with feeling, the feeling flowing with the music and the breeze from the curtains, the feeling colored by the blue flowers painted in a border around the walls" (p. 103). Nightswan's passion introduces him to a new vitality; as she "moved under him, her rhythm merging into the sound of the wind shaking the rafters and the sound of the rain in the trees" (p. 104).

Through Nightswan, Tayo feels the power of wind and rain penetrate human and natural landscape. Just before he leaves her room, he stands in the doorway "aware of the damp earth smell outside." She tells him: "You don't have to understand what is happening. But remember this day. You will recognize it later. You are part of it now" (p. 105). Through the memory of his encounter with Nightswan, Tayo begins to heal. Life rhythms flow into him.

Tayo has returned home broken by the detached brutality of World War II a number of years after his encounter with Nightswan. Wandering among old haunts, he sits on the porch outside her remembered room. That music and those white curtains, the wind and her locust blossom perfume, are gone. But he learns something important there on the cracked porch of remembrance:

> The place felt good; he leaned back against the wall until its surface pushed against his backbone solidly. He picked up a fragment of fallen plaster and drew dusty white stripes across the backs of his hands, the way ceremonial dancers sometimes did, except they used white clay and not old plaster. . . . He rubbed it carefully across his light brown skin . . . and then he knew why it was done by the dancers: it connected him to the earth. (p. 109)

Tayo learns through this woman's flesh to feel his own connectedness, so that the place bears her presence in his remembering their time together, the space of memory sensual and earthen.

Through Betonie the medicine man, Tayo learns to be at home with and connected to the sky, as well as the earth. The ceremony conducted for Tayo by Betonie forms the healing center of Silko's book. Here Tayo is able to participate in symbolic events and mythic space, the action of the novel as a whole woven from many temporal dimensions, including the non-time or pretime of the emergence, creation, and origin stories structuring the ceremony. Tayo's integration into the Laguna community occurs through a ceremony which simultaneously provides a kind of paradigm for political consciousness.

—Reyes García, "Senses of Place in *Ceremony*," *MELUS* 10, no. 4 (Winter 1983): 40–41

ANDREW WIGET

By creating a narrative structure ⟨for *Ceremony*⟩ that, like Tayo's consciousness, integrates an initially fragmented presentation into a coherent, linear narrative, Silko transforms not just Tayo's story but her narrator's telling into a ceremonial event, framed by sunrise prayers and motivated by the assertion that she is telling us the story that Thought-Woman, the Creator, is thinking. Because of the convertibility of the roles of patient and medicine man ⟨. . .⟩, the novel implies that several such stories and ceremonies are embedded within it. In the end, Tayo's story, through the agency of the narrator, becomes for us our ceremony of reading and, in restoring some of our shared humanity despite our cultural differences, offers us a healing equal to Tayo's.

The power of the mythic perspective to shape our experience of the world is also at the heart of Silko's short fiction, which she has collected with her poetry in *Storyteller* (1980). The title story is about an Eskimo woman who shares her hut with an old man who makes passes at her when he is not mumbling a story about a polar bear that has turned to stalk the hunter pursuing it. Anxious for other company, she flirts with local whites, but is brought to disgust when a sexual encounter turns into a nightmare and to hatred when she learns that the local trader had poisoned her parents. She exploits the man's lust by leading him out onto thin ice, where he drowns in the river. In "Yellow Woman" a young Laguna woman meets a Navajo down by the river while she is getting water; when he addresses her as Yellow Woman, she begins to wonder whether she is indeed living out a myth in latter times, and he, of course, does nothing to disabuse her of the ideas. Witchery is central to "Tony's Story," which, like Simon Ortiz's "The Killing of the State Cop" and perhaps the trial scene from *House Made of Dawn*, is based on the actual murder of a policeman by two Acoma youths who perceived him to be a witch. Silko's achievement lies in realizing more fully than any of her contemporaries the possibilities of Native American myths and the storytelling frame, not just for ethnographic "local color" or even for a context of allusion, but for providing the vital principle for plot construction and characterization.

—Andrew Wiget, *Native American Literature* (Boston: Twayne Publishers, 1985), 89–90

KRISTIN HERZOG

The style of the novel ⟨*Ceremony*⟩ superbly expresses the essence of the story. It is often as fragmentary as Tayo's mental condition and as disjointed as the tribe's position between cultural persistence and assimilation. Past and future are telescoped into the present. Flashbacks and dream visions contribute to the reader's feeling of disruption as well as of a continual challenge to do what Tayo instinctively tries to do, that is, weave together the fragments, struggle to find a pattern of meaning. What differentiates Silko's style from that of most Anglo-American novelists is her use of oral traditions which are intricately woven into the narrative in the form of poems, ritual prayers, stories, and tribal rumors.

The subtle portrayal of gender roles and gender traits in this novel is partly reflected in its style. Psychologists have told us in recent years that woman's mode of thinking is more contextual, more narrative, more personal, and more open-ended than man's more formal, abstract, and goal-directed thought, and similar observations have been made about woman's style of writing. Even if these theories are discounted as vague or unproven, the difference between a rational, linear, and abstract style and a visionary, circular, or emotive one can be described as "more masculine" or "more feminine" respectively, without contending that they can be used by male or female authors only. Silko's style is to a large extent "feminine" in these terms. It is fragmentary, poetic, ritualistic, and its essence is story in the sense of tribal tale or rumor, of what in Western terms would be called "old wives' tales," superstitious women's gossip not worth paying attention to in a male-structured society. Silko has stated in an interview that she bases her fiction not on Laguna stories the way ethnologists report them in print: "I don't have to because from the time I was little I heard quite a bit. I heard it in what would be passed off now as rumor or gossip" ⟨Sun Tracks, 1976, 30⟩. In an essay about the healing and comforting power of stories, she writes, "We make no distinctions between the stories—whether they are history, whether they are fact, whether they are gossip" ⟨"Language and Literature from a Pueblo Indian Perspective," 1981, 60⟩. However, Silko interweaves these free associations of tribal rumors, fragments of history, and ritual songs with a more linear, novelistic narrative, a more "masculine" element of style, thereby creating balance and vitality of expression. Also, the stories she uses are often not old wives' tales, but old men's tales. An example of the latter is one of the introductory poems ⟨in which . . . . ⟩ we find an old man "pregnant" with stories like a woman with child. The novel ends on a similar note: Tayo has been healed and has matured to the point of being able to tell the old men of the tribe his story. Stories among Native Americans, whether in the form of gossip or elaborate ritual, dream or factual narrative, are never old wives' tales in the Western sense. They are the essence of survival because they build community; they tie the individual to common roots and common hopes. "Story . . . substantiates life, continues it, and creates it." Men as well as women have to give birth in this way. Silko's stylistic devices of blending mythical and rational, circular and linear elements correspond to the balance of male and female traits in her characters, and they challenge the reader to question Western ways of portraying gender.

—Kristin Herzog, "Thinking Woman and Feeling Man: Gender in Silko's *Ceremony*," *MELUS* 12, no. 1 (Spring 1985): 26–27

ELIZABETH N. EVASDAUGHTER

In *Ceremony*, Leslie Silko brilliantly crosses racial styles of humor in order to cure the foolish delusions readers may have, if we think we are superior to Indians or inferior to whites, or perhaps superior to whites or inferior to Indians. Silko plays off affectionate Pueblo humor against the black humor so prominent in 20th-century white culture. This comic strategy has the end-result of opening our eyes to our general foolishness, and also to the possibility of combining the merits of all races. Joseph Campbell wrote in *The Inner Reaches of Outer Space* of the change in mythologies away from the local and tribal toward a mythology that will arise from "this unified earth as of one harmonious being" (16–17). *Ceremony* is a work that changes local mythologies in that more inclusive spirit. ⟨. . .⟩

All the instances of Indian humor in *Ceremony* have been overlooked by some of the white readers I have talked with, possibly because of lack of contact with non-European communities or culture. Indian irony can be "either so subtle or so keyed to an understanding from within of what is funny to a people that an outsider would fail to recognize it" ⟨Joseph Bruchac, "Striking the Pole," 1987, 23⟩. Such outsiders tend to take many light passages in *Ceremony* as solemn or tense, and wear themselves out before the real crisis comes. Yet Silko has given non-Indian readers enough clues to enjoy her inside jokes. Although she grew up on the Laguna Pueblo reservation, she is familiar with our European culture, as she has correctly called it. She went to white schools, and she has read Steinbeck, Faulkner, Poe, Borges, and Flannery O'Connor, some with great interest, others with fascination ⟨Per Seyersted, "Two Interviews with Leslie Marmon Silko," 1981, 22⟩. She understands this culture so well that she has been able to play with European black humor, which responds, not to the beautiful blackness of the black people, of nighttime outdoors, or of the forest shadows; the blackness involved in black humor is the darkness of opposition to light. Silko splits black humor as she did the spirit of Winter. She delineates one type of black humor, characterized by Emo, which bases its world view on black or unrelieved hatred and acts as the agent of hatred. She deploys a second type of black humor related to the irony of Indian ritual clowns, characterized by Tayo and Betonie, which includes hatred and white oppression in its world view without allowing them to monopolize the world. The former blackness enjoys the degradation of others; the second jokes about degrading things as they are, but shouldn't be. The first is death-dealing; the second, death-paralyzing.

—Elizabeth N. Evasdaughter, "Leslie Marmon Silko's *Ceremony*: Healing Ethnic Hatred by Mixed-Breed Laughter," *MELUS* 15, no. 1 (Spring 1988): 83, 88–89

PAULA GUNN ALLEN

Ceremony is a novel that I find particularly troublesome, and I tend to non-teach it, if you can picture such a thing. I focus on the story, the plot and action. I read the novel quite differently from how it is read by many. I believe I could no more do (or sanction) the kind of ceremonial investigation of *Ceremony* done by some researchers than I could slit my mother's throat. Even seeing some of it published makes my skin crawl. I have yet to read one of those articles all the way through, my physical reaction is so pronounced.

I teach the novel as being about a half-breed, in the context of half-breed literature from *Cogewea* on. Certainly that is how I read the novel the first time I read it—as a plea for inclusion by a writer who felt excluded and compelled to depict the potential importance of breeds to Laguna survival. The parts of the novel that set other pulses atremble largely escape me. The long poem text that runs through the center has always seemed to me to contribute little to the story or its understanding. Certainly the salvation of Laguna from drought is one of its themes, but the Tayo stories which, I surmise, form their own body of literature would have been a better choice if Silko's ⟨intention⟩ was to clarify or support her text with traditional materials.

Tayo is the name of one of the dramatic characters around Keresland. Perhaps in some story I am unfamiliar with, he is involved with Fly or Reed Woman. But the story she lays alongside the novel is a clan story, and is not to be told outside of the clan.

I have long wondered why she did so. Certainly, being raised in greater proximity to Laguna village than I, she must have been told what I was, that we don't tell these things outside. Perhaps her desire to demonstrate the importance of breeds led her to this, or perhaps no one ever told her why the Lagunas and other Pueblos are so closed about their spiritual activities and the allied oral tradition.

Two instructive events were used as a reference to convey to me what behavior was expected with regard to passing on Laguna materials. I was told that an anthropologist, Elsie Clews Parsons, had come to Laguna to collect material for her study of Pueblo religion and social culture. They had given her information readily enough and everything seemed fine. But when Parsons published the material, Lagunas saw how she treated their practices and beliefs, and they were horrified. In accordance with her academic training, she objectified, explained, detailed and analyzed their lives as though they were simply curios, artifacts, fetishes, and discussed the supernaturals as though they were objects of interest and patronization. Her underlying attitude for the supernaturals, the sacred, and the people who honored them didn't evade notice. The Lagunas were "red-haired" as my mother would say. Coincidently (or not so coincidently) the terrible drought deepened—the same drought Silko depicts in *Ceremony*—and in its wake many other ills visited the Pueblo. Personal horrors and society-wide horrors ensued; the discovery of uranium on Laguna land, not far from where the giantess's head and her headless body had been flung by the War Twins, the development of nuclear weapons near Jemez, the Second World War, jackpile mine, water and land poisoned by nuclear waste, the village of Paguate all but surrounded by tailing-mesas almost as perfectly formed as the natural mesas all around. It's hardly any wonder that they shut it down. All entry by non-traditionals to dances and stories was cut off. They witnessed first-hand the appalling consequences of telling what was private for reasons that far exceed simple cultural purism.

While Silko details these horrors in *Ceremony*, she does not attribute them to security leaks. She is poignantly aware of the closure of village life to outsiders and depicts the pain such exclusion brings; she is aware of the discovery of the uranium used to bomb Hiroshima and Nagasaki, she is aware of the devastating drought, the loss of self that the entire Pueblo suffered in those years, yet she is unaware of one small but essential bit of information: the information that telling the old stories, revealing the old ways can only lead to disaster.

—Paula Gunn Allen, "Special Problems in Teaching Leslie Marmon Silko's *Ceremony*," *The American Indian Quarterly* 14, no. 4 (Fall 1990): 382–84

EDITH SWAN

Among the mythologies of many American Indian societies, tales reporting ceremonies, myths and ritual dwell on the character of a "Culture Hero." ⟨In "Mythology and Values," 1957, Katherine⟩ Spencer presents a cogent synthesis of the series of events in which the hero commonly engages, a sequence which I have annotated with reference to the personnel and plot of *Ceremony*:

> Typically, the hero experiences a series of misfortunes in which he needs supernatural assistance if he is to survive. Sometimes he precipitates the misadventure himself by actively courting danger or intentionally disregarding prohibitions; . . . *behind the hero's seeming passivity in suffering catastrophe the stories show a deep preoccupation with his active responsibility* for provoking the mishaps that plague him [cursing the rain]. *Rejection by his family* [Auntie and his Mother] or *ridicule and scorn* on the part of associates [Emo] may set the stage for the hero's reckless behavior. His misadventures usually occur during *sexual or hunting exploits* [The War might be counted here as well as his relationship with Night Swan, Ts'eh, the Hunter and Mountain Lion] . . . The hero's misadventures are usually bodily attack or capture by animals, natural phenomenon, supernaturals, or aliens. They may *leave him ill, destroyed bodily, transformed* [Coyote Witchery], or stranded in an inac-

cessible place. In this predicament the supernaturals come to his rescue or protect him from further harm. *They restore him by ritual treatment* [Ku'oosh and Betonie] *and from contact with them he acquires ceremonial knowledge and power. Usually it is the restoration ceremony performed over him as the patient that he learns in all its details* [Betonie and Shush] . . . With each misadventure and restoration he gains in . . . ritual knowledge and power of his own *to be able to protect himself* [Star map on war shield] with little or no help from supernaturals. In the final events of the story the *hero returns to his own people* [story in Kiva and family], without resentment for whatever part they may have played in his misadventures. (Spencer 19, emphasis added)

In the novel, Tayo displays the attributes normally assigned to the Culture Hero as a mythic archetype ⟨Paul Radin, *The Trickster*, 1956, 46–53, 166–69⟩. Without question, Silko has crafted her hero in this time-honored persona so popular to native storytelling traditions, showing Tayo's metamorphosis from being a wastrel to his status as a full-fledged hero.

Moreover, to a Laguna youngster, the name "Tayo" would be as familiar as Superman or Batman is to a white child. *He is a traditional folklore hero.* His story tells of being taken to the sky by his pet eagle, and in flight he sings and the people see him. They go to the mountain at the zenith in the upper world where he goes "northward down" to the home of Spider Woman, then hunts with her grandsons snaring robins to procure a gift for her. He stays for a while. ⟨. . .⟩

In ⟨Franz⟩ Boas' collection entitled *Keresan Texts*, he comments that Tayo's words are Hopi; furthermore, he notes that originally this was a Hopi tale (146, 229) brought to Laguna presumably along with many other elements derived from Hopi and Zuni. If so, Silko named her hero after a borrowed Laguna mythic hero who at a minimum flies on wings of eagles, sings in Hopi and lives with Spider Woman. In addition, the status of the folklore Tayo may have been enhanced by belonging to a Hopi story, a people reputed to be sophisticated and spiritually prominent among the Western Pueblos, exemplifying how cultural admixture is recognized and incorporated into Laguna mythology.

—Edith Swan, "Laguna Prototypes of Manhood in *Ceremony*," *MELUS* 17, no. 1 (Spring 1991–92): 45–46

DONNA PERRY

⟨Interview with Leslie Marmon Silko by Donna Perry⟩

LS: ⟨In writing *Almanac of the Dead*,⟩ I was thinking about trying to do something completely different with the novel as a genre. The Mayan almanacs had really strong images that are often repeated. And since a lot of the remnants covered war, destruction, politics, war, destruction, politics, I thought that my almanac is going to be crammed full of narratives. That's what you can do with any kind of almanac, whether it's a Mayan almanac or a farmer's almanac. Old almanacs had all kinds of information and details and stories, stuff you just wonder, Why would this be here—except that it's a part of the time. But I didn't write the novel the way it's put together.

DP: How was it written?

LS: It was written the way you would make a film. A lot of it was written as narratives. I didn't expect them all to so interconnect. I suppose I expected it to be more mysterious and fragmented. More destroyed. Maybe more like the old Mayan almanacs were. But it did something that I didn't plan and I would have been afraid to hope for: It did all finally fit together. That's all *Ceremony* is: You just build, and your pieces are narratives.

There are four or five different books in there. Someone said I could have split them out, but I said, "No, we're not making tidy little books." But also I was resisting writing a book that's so radical. At some point I had to say, "Oh my God, here go all of the aesthetics of the novel, all the rules." Luckily the genre has very few rules, comparatively. But I was horrified.

DP: Besides form, the content is so radical.

LS: Yeah, I asked myself, "Do I really have to write about all this incredible twisted sexual torture? Do I have to write about America's fascination with blood and violent death?" But I knew I had to because nobody really wants to talk about it. I had to connect that with Christianity and the Holy Eucharist and the Church and the Inquisition. And I knew people weren't going to like it, but I had to do it.

DP: You say you had to tell this story. Why? To lay out what happened to the native peoples? Or to grab ahold of the white middle-class readers who were going to buy the book and shake them by the shoulders and say, "Hey idiots, wake up"?

LS: This is my 763-page indictment for five hundred years of theft, murder, pillage, and rape. So is *Almanac* long? Sure, but federal indictments are long. The one returned against Charles Keating, who took one billion dollars just in one savings and loan in Arizona, is long. And mine is a little more interesting reading than a straight-on legal indictment. ⟨. . .⟩

When I handed in the manuscript to Michael Korda at Simon and Schuster, he understood the spirit of what I was trying to do. He did work with the Hungarian freedom fighters in the fifties. But it didn't have the chapter names, and it wasn't broken into the geographical sections. So it was still happening when I handed it to him.

And he said it was this daunting monolith of prose. "We've got to do something to help the reader," he said. And I said, "I'll help the reader all I can." And he said, "Well, could we break it into chapters?" And then I got really excited because it reminded me again about how almanacs have all these little short sections. I've collected all kinds of almanacs over time.

When we started editing there was an instant where we could have edited it to be more of a best-seller and actually pulled whole books out of it. But I knew that the damn thing was an almanac. We did cut about 350 pages. I did most of the cuts, although Michael did make suggestions. It took us both a while to figure out what the book wanted to be.

DP: When you saw that it was going to be an almanac, what difference did that make?

LS: Then I started to think about the notion of time reckoned not with numerals and numbers, but what if you just talk about time as narratives, day by day. What happened that day is the identity of the day. More in the direction of what the Mayans thought. Once we did that, the editing went differently, and it became a whole different book.

   —Donna Perry, *Backtalk: Women Writers Speak Out* (New Brunswick: Rutgers University Press, 1993), 326–28

J. BROWDY DE HERNANDEZ

The traditional "Yellow Woman" stories that are written into Silko's *Storyteller* ⟨. . . are⟩ resistant to by-the-book Euramerican feminist readings. In one version, "Buffalo Story," it is a time of famine for the people when Kochininako is seduced by Buffalo Man, who carries her far away to his country. Kochininako's husband, Arrowboy, pursues them, and takes her back with him, followed by the whole herd of angry "Buffalo People." Arrowboy shoots Buffalo Man and all the other buffalo, and is glad because now the people will have food. But Kochininako is sad, because she loved Buffalo Man, and when Arrowboy sees that he kills her too. "I killed her / because she wanted to stay with the Buffalo People / she wanted to go with them / and now she is with them," he tells her father (75). The people go to dry the buffalo meat and bring it home, and the story ends by informing us that Kochininako's love for

Buffalo Man saved her people from starvation, and began the tradition of going East to hunt buffalo:

> It was all because
> one time long ago
> our daughter, our sister Kochininako
> went away with them (76).

It is possible, and even tempting, to read such stories through a feminist frame of reference, arguing that they show indigenous support for the free sexuality of women and for the ability of women to act as the agents of their own stories, even when these go against tribal customs of marriage. But asked in an interview if she would support such a reading, Silko strongly objects. The interviewer asks: "Do you see the myths concerning her [Yellow Woman] as having arisen from the need for escape on the part of the women from a kind of social and sexual domination?" Silko replies:

> No, not at all. The need for that kind of escape is the need of a
> woman in middle-America, a white Anglo, the WASP woman. . . .
> The kinds of things that cause white upper-middle-class women to
> flee the home for awhile to escape . . . domination and powerlessness
> and inferior status, vis-a-vis the husband, and the male, those kinds of
> forces are not operating . . . . What's operating in those stories of
> Kochininako is this attraction, this passion, this connection between
> the human world and the animal and spirit worlds 〈Kim Barnes, "A
> Leslie Marmon Silko Interview," 1986, 97〉.

Silko's response illustrates the danger of imposing an alien theoretical structure on any given story. Just as it would be misleading to use the Native theory of the link between the natural and human worlds to explain a Western scientific paper, it is misleading to try to use feminist analysis to explain Yellow Woman's motives. Yellow Woman, as Silko reminds us, comes from a matrilineal society in which "the women have called the shots pretty much in the world of relationships and in the everyday world . . . . the female, the mother, is a real powerful person, and much more the authority figure [than the man]" (Barnes, "Interview," 97). We are not wrong in understanding Kochininako as a powerful, independent woman, then, only in imagining her power against the backdrop of a patriarchal culture that she opposes. *Storyteller*, in a non-militant but very firm way, demonstrates the danger of reading Native American women's texts by the light of Western feminist universalism.

—J. Browdy de Hernandez, "Writing (for) Survival: Continuity and Change in Four Contemporary Native American Women's Autobiographies," *Wicazo Sa Review* 10, no. 2 (Fall 1994): 48–50

JANE SEQUOYA-MAGDALENO

Popular identification with Indianness as a symbolic site of resistance conceptually linked to idealisms of the organic revived with the countercultural movement of the 1960s, creating a receptive climate for Leslie Marmon Silko's first novel, *Ceremony*, in 1977. The author, of Laguna Pueblo, Anglo, Mexican, and "mixed-blood Plains" heritage, was acclaimed by Frank MacShane in the *New York Times Book Review* as "the most accomplished Indian writer of her generation." *Ceremony* is a syncretic work characterized by the incorporation of fragments from traditional Pueblo and Navajo clan stories that signify at once a home base to which the pathologically decentered protagonist may return and the Indianness of the genre. However, at the same time that it redefines Indianness in terms of cultural syncretism, *Ceremony* novelizes the "residue of a broken ensemble" (Lacoue-Labarthe and Nancy, *The Literary Absolute*, 39–58) in keeping with the metynomic "model . . . of fragmented antiquity, the landscape of ruins" (50). Thus, the formal method of Silko's justly celebrated work is that of a double appropriation of disparate evaluative codes that are in some respects complementary and in others incommensurable: it adapts the secular form of the modern novel to reproduce elements of sacred Pueblo and Navajo oral cycles at the same time that it invokes the stylistic form of the oral tradition (a device that is one of the earliest conventions of the novel form) to represent the dramatic conflict and resolution most characteristic of Western narrative.

The dual positioning of the work in mainstream (assimilative) and tribal (exclusive) societies creates a number of problems for its critical reception; yet, rather than being addressed, those problems are generally circumvented by the essence-seeking project of multicultural canon formation. Although Silko ostensibly writes against the grain of the "Vanishing American" motif of North American Indian iconography, the premise of the unreformed Indian as the residue of history enters *Ceremony* under cover of a binary relationship between "mixed-blood" and "full-blood"; the former signifies survival of tradition in adaptive developmental forms, and the latter its stagnation, degeneration, and corruption—thus inverting the nineteenth-century North American motif of the "tragic mixed-blood."

However, insofar as Silko's compensatory strategy defines as residual a population already "minorized," that is, construed by the mainstream imagination as categorically "minor" (an effect of its prior representation in terms of a primitive stage in the universal history of civilization), it not only reproduces the conventions of discourse of Indianness but legitimates those conventions as a Native American revitalization movement. Hence, despite a proliferation of commentary on *Ceremony*, there has been substantial resistance to critiquing its form of representation. ⟨. . .⟩

Ceremony is a canonical work in the sense not only that it is one of the most frequently assigned novels in university classes today (in both "literary" and "nonliterary" courses that need to cite/site "Indianness"), but also that it has generated within Native American literary criticism a sort of parallel universe, reproducing within the academic arena the primary concern of the text—a struggle between contesting systems of power and knowledge. At issue in that struggle, as it is taken up by pedagogical multiculturalism, are the emergent institutional interests of Indian-identified cultural producers to define and control the signifier "Indian."

That these interests only gesturally coincide with those of less privileged Native Americans is a contradiction that is generally suppressed by the legitimating strategies of national canon formation. To the extent that critical reception of Silko's *Ceremony* reenacts the novel's thematic concern to redefine Indian identity according to the interests of the most acculturated class, it can be read as an allegory of crises in contemporary culture arising out of confrontations between conflicting worldviews to which writers of Native American fiction are particularly sensitive.

—Jane Sequoya-Magdaleno, "Telling the *Différance*: Representations of Identity in the Discourse of Indianness," in *The Ethnic Canon: Histories, Institutions, and Interventions*, ed. David Palumbo-Liu (Minneapolis: University of Minnesota Press, 1995), 92–93

STUART COCHRAN

The land pervades writing of the southwest as both a physical and a figurative reality—an originary place and a living presence. The Native American writers Leslie Marmon Silko and Simon Ortiz and the Chicano writers Rudolfo Anaya and Jimmy Santiago Baca speak of identities inseparable from particular landscapes and of the spiritually and culturally disintegrative impact of the loss of that connection. At the same time, they insist on the primacy of storytelling and the significance that stories give to the land and its people. Silko and Anaya suggest that cultural identity arises on a field that is *both* essential and constructed. Their ethnicity is in part a heightened sensitivity to a homeland as it is learned through stories which attribute meaning to and through the land. ⟨. . .⟩

⟨. . .⟩ The parallels that Silko sees ⟨in *Ceremony*⟩ between the nuclear testing assault on the earth at White Sands, the contamination of traditional Pueblo land, stories and ways of seeing, and the bombing of Hiroshima and Nagasaki emphasize the tragic possibility of humankind's common fate under the white destroyers' witchery. Silko is suggesting the universality of her healing ceremony beyond the particular restoration and reintegration of Tayo into his world. Memory, stories, and a renewed reverence for the land are at the crux of the revision she proposes for the non-Native American reader, as well—the necessary praxis of ecocriticism. *Ceremony* joins an aboriginal manifestation of what Aldo Leopold calls the "land ethic" ⟨*A Sand County Almanac*, 1970, 237⟩ with the process of history.

Silko's effort to reconcile the restoration of a particular landscape with a universal revision provokes the question of whether *Ceremony* itself—the story—is generative of healing, as a social constructionist might hold the story is generative of Tayo's ethnic identity. Although these two aspects of *Ceremony* are not strictly homologous, we can see how essentialism and constructionism are both implicated in the text when we identify the levels on which the novel engages us.

The construction of *Ceremony*'s narrative and the reconstruction of Tayo's individual identity out of the Laguna Pueblo ethnic identity present at least three levels for consideration. There is a story in which a particular landscape is essential to a protagonist's quest for an identity (Tayo's and perhaps any Laguna Pueblo's). There is a story in which a particular landscape may be essential to a storyteller's communal voice as her experience is constructed (Ts'its'tsi'nako's thought process) and as she constructs her narrative—a semi-mediated experience in which Silko knows the landscape both from being there and from the cultural stories which give "there" its identity. And there is a story in which a particular landscape is entirely mediated figuratively to a reader who has never been "there" and may never be "there" but can relate to the figurative landscape as a symbol of a universal landscape.

Since the last case operates on the level of pure construction—narrative figuration—to a reader, no particular landscape is essential to the story's symbolic power, albeit the significance of Trinity Site is inestimable. The first and second cases, however, are more problematic, since a cultural identity has arisen in and around a particular landscape and has constructed a storyteller who constructs a story which is (and has always been) constructing a culture. And part of that "cultural work" is precisely a return to the land: a reclamation of the originary space, literally and spiritually. William Bevis identifies this "Homing In" theme as the most characteristic of contemporary Native American novels:

> Most Native American novels are not "eccentric," centrifugal, diverging, expanding [characteristics of the "leaving home" plots of American "classics"], but "incentric," centripetal, converging, contracting. The hero comes home . . . . In Native American novels, coming home, staying put, contracting, even what we call "regressing" to a place, a past where one has been before, is not only the primary story, it is a Primary mode of knowledge and a primary good.
> ⟨"Native American Novels," 1987, 582⟩

If coming home or staying there is "a primary good," we cannot discount the importance of a particular tribal landscape to the "cultural construal of descent" ⟨*Ethnic Change*, 1981, 5⟩ by theorizing it away in the analysis of larger historical forces, since such an approach demeans the Native American experience it purports to explain.

    —Stuart Cochran, "The Ethnic Implications of Stories, Spirits, and the Land in Native American Pueblo and Aztlán Writing," *MELUS* 20, no. 2 (Summer 1995): 70, 79–80

B I B L I O G R A P H Y

Laguna Woman. 1974.
Ceremony. 1977.
Storyteller. 1981.
With the Delicacy and Strength of Lace. 1985.
Almanac of the Dead. 1991.
Sacred Water. 1993.
Yellow Woman and a Beauty of the Spirit: Essays on Native American Life Today. 1996.

SARAH WINNEMUCCA
1844–1891

SARAH WINNEMUCCA, also known as Sarah Hopkins and as Thocmetony, was born about 1844, in what would now be Nevada, near Humboldt Lake. Her tribe, the Northern Paiutes (or Piutes), roamed western Nevada, northeastern California, and southern Oregon following antelope herds and gathering food. Sarah grew up during a troubled time for the Paiutes: by the 1850s, gold had been discovered in California and increasing numbers of whites were making their way through Paiute territory. White settlements brought diseases with them, and their cattle devoured the grasses that had supported the antelope herds. Sarah's grandfather, Captain Truckee, is said to have guided John C. Fremont across the Sierra Nevada to California in 1845; perhaps due to his experiences with Fremont, Truckee determined that his tribe would follow a path of peaceful coexistence with whites. Sarah consequently grew up among both Paiutes and whites and learned to speak fluent English and Spanish. In 1860, she briefly attended a Catholic school in San Jose, California, but she was forced to leave after less than a month when wealthy white parents objected to an Indian child attending school with their children.

At about this time, the Paiutes began to realize that they were being cheated by corrupt Indian agents, and tensions between whites and Indians started to escalate. These tensions erupted in armed conflicts in 1865, in which one of Sarah's young brothers died. For several years after this, she served as interpreter for the soldiers posted at Camp McDermit, in northeastern Nevada. In 1878, a war broke out between the Bannock tribe of Idaho and the white army. Although some Paiutes joined the Bannocks, others did not, and Winnemucca herself offered her services to the army as an interpreter, guide, and scout. After the Bannock war, both the Paiute and the Bannock tribes—regardless of their participation in the war—were removed from their land and exiled to the Yakima Reservation.

As a result of this unjust act, Winnemucca became a more public figure. She traveled to San Francisco to lecture on behalf of the Paiutes. Her lectures led to an invitation to Washington, D.C., in 1880, so that she might state her case before the president. After this, Winnemucca traveled extensively in the East, giving over three hundred speeches on behalf of the Indians and protesting the wrongs of the federal Indian policies.

From Winnemucca's lectures and speeches came *Life Among the Piutes: Their Wrongs and Claims* (1883), the first known work published in English by a Native American woman. A combination of tribal history, personal narrative, and political tract, the book was designed to make white readers support the cause of the Indians; it even contained a petition that readers could send to Congress. Despite Winnemucca's efforts, however, the government did not alter its policy towards the Paiutes.

In 1884, Winnemucca returned to Nevada to start a school for Indian children, where they could learn in their own languages. After four years, however, the school closed, and Winnemucca went to live with her sister in Idaho; there she died, in 1891. Although her efforts on behalf of the Paiutes and other tribes were not ultimately successful, she was an important educator and diplomat and was, at the time of her death, considered "the most famous Indian woman of the Pacific Coast."

CRITICAL EXTRACTS

CATHERINE S. FOWLER

Sarah's book is principally an autobiographical and historical account of the period 1844 through 1883, while her article is essentially a statement on pre-contact ethnography. The coverage of cultural data in Sarah's article parallels in many ways the ethnographic paradigm in early anthropology. She provides data on Northern Paiute subsistence patterns, trade, shamanism, puberty observances, courting and marriage customs, death and burial practices, and more. Some of these topics are also given expanded treatment in her book. Sarah's description of antelope charming and hunting is particularly detailed, perhaps because her father, Old Winnemucca, had antelope power and she witnessed the procedure several times ⟨Hopkins 1883: *Life Among the Piutes: Their Wrongs and Claims*: 55 ff.⟩.

Both Sarah's book and her article also contain valuable data on her perceptions of the cultural and attitudinal changes she felt were occurring during this period. For example, she suggests that less stability exists in Northern Paiute marriages than existed formerly:

> They take a woman now without much ado, as white people do, and
> leave them oftener than of old . . . an indulgence taken advantage of

> to abandon an old wife and secure a younger one. They argue that it
> is better for them to do so than to leave their young women for the
> temptation of white men. (Hopkins 1882:255)

In another example, she notes that native doctors are beginning to "know their value," to have more political power and to extract money fees from patients in emulation of White doctors. There are numerous suggestions of other changes as well.

Subtle courtesies, assumptions and values are also portrayed in Sarah's materials. For example, she speaks of always making a place for a weary guest to sit, making a fire to warm him or her and offering the person something to eat (Hopkins 1883:12). She also describes the decision-making process by which everyone gets an opportunity to speak and think about matters before deciding on an issue (ibid., 27). Differences in values held by Whites and Paiutes are also discussed; for example, Sarah's attempt to make Old Winnemucca understand that it is often the sincere custom of Whites to give gifts to friends when they depart. Old Winnemucca was very hesitant to take Agent Sam Parrish's gifts when Parrish was relieved at Malheur because they would be painful reminders of his absence. Similarly, Old Winnemucca reasoned, one keeps nothing that belongs to the dead (ibid., 52). In another passage, Sarah also explains to the people the peculiar White custom of hanging clothes on a line to dry. This did not mean, she adds, that they were being thrown away and were free for the taking. Indians had been shot in Virginia city for "stealing" laundry (ibid., 120).

From all accounts, Sarah's speeches also contained considerable ethnographic material. In fact, one might speculate that perhaps more was known about Northern Paiute ethnography by the general public in the 1880's partly through Sarah's efforts than has been known at any time since.

One of the most interesting features of Sarah's book, and, I suspect one of the most important for interpreting it, is its narrative style. Her tale is told with numerous quotes from participants, although, quite obviously by reconstruction. I suspect that this may be the same quotative style that is a major feature of Northern Paiute narratives. Sarah's book is, perhaps, her narrative tale, her view of the history of her family and the difficulties of her people— her ethnohistory. As such, from our point of view, it contains some errors of historical fact (although considering the many names and dates, and the amount of detail, it is remarkably accurate). In line with this reasoning, it is interesting to compare Sarah's account with those by other authors in the same period. ⟨. . .⟩ From the academic perspective, her book lacks the balance of historical evaluation that scholarly models would suggest. However, placed in the more appropriate context of Northern Paiute oral tradition, her account would be balanced by those of other narrators—a context that it loses in print. Accusations of bias and error may result from attempts to judge her work according to another model.

The book's narrative style, as well as some of its ethnographic subtleties, lead me to conclude that while some of Sarah's contemporaries questioned the fact, the book is primarily her effort and not that of Mary Mann. Although Mann undoubtedly edited the book for sentence structure, spelling and punctuation, as she freely states in her preface, it could only be Sarah's detractors that would suggest that she were not capable of the achievement.

—Catherine S. Fowler, "Sarah Winnemucca," in *American Indian Intellectuals*, ed. Margot Liberty (St. Paul: West Publishing Co., 1978), 39–40

GAE WHITNEY CANFIELD

When Sarah arrived in Boston, Elizabeth ⟨Palmer Peabody⟩ was seventy-nine years old and had suffered a slight stroke but she soon began working assiduously for the cause of the "Princess" Sarah Winnemucca. She proposed that Sarah give a series of lectures, so that subscribers would learn the history and culture of the Paiutes as well as their present circumstances. When Sarah found that she could cover only a few points in each lecture, she became determined to write about her people at length. Elizabeth was willing to see that the book was published. It would be a means of introducing Sarah and her cause and also would bring in revenue.

Thus Sarah gained innumerable speaking engagements up and down the East Coast before large church gatherings and Indian Association groups. She brought a new awareness to her audiences of the plight of the American Indian: their lack of land, sustenance, citizenship, and the rights that go with citizenship. She reminded her audiences that the Indians had no representation in the United States government.

Sarah lectured in New York, Connecticut, Rhode Island, Maryland, Massachusetts, and Pennsylvania within the first few months of her stay in the East. She enjoyed creating a dramatic impression, dressed in fringed buckskin and beads, with armlets and bracelets adorning her arms and wrists. She even included the affectation of a gold crown on her head and a wampum bag of velvet, decorated with an embroidered cupid, hanging from her waist. ⟨. . .⟩

One early lecture in Boston was intended for women only. Sarah spoke of the domestic education given by Paiute grandmothers to the youth of both sexes concerning their relations with each other before and after marriage. It was "a lecture which never failed to excite the moral enthusiasm of every woman that heard it," according to Elizabeth. The elderly woman was convinced by Sarah that the Paiutes' education of their young was based on "natural religion and family moralities."

As well as lecturing, Sarah found time to write *Life Among the Piutes: Their Wrongs and Claims*, the story of her own life arranged in eight chapters. In the book she made the Paiute woman's position in councils and family life sound somewhat liberated: "The women know as much as the men do, and their advice is often asked. We have a republic as well as you. The council-tent is our Congress, and anybody can speak who has anything to say, women and all." She described how women were quite willing to go into battle alongside their husbands, if need be.

⟨Elizabeth's sister, Mary Mann,⟩ offered to edit Sarah's manuscript and found it difficult work. She wrote a friend:

> I wish you could see her manuscript as a matter of curiosity. I don't
> think the English language ever got such a treatment before. I have to
> recur to her sometimes to know what a word is, as spelling is an
> unknown quantity to her, as you mathematicians would express it.
> She often takes syllables off of words & adds them or rather prefixes
> them to other words, but the story is heart-breaking, and told with a
> simplicity & eloquence that cannot be described, for it is not high-
> faluting eloquence, tho' sometimes it lapses into verse (and quite
> poetical verse too). I was always considered fanatical about Indians,
> but I have a wholly new conception of them now, and we civilized
> people may well stand abashed before their purity of life & their
> truthfulness.

—Gae Whitney Canfield, *Sarah Winnemucca of the Northern Paiutes* (Norman, OK: University of Oklahoma Press, 1983), 200–3

H. David Brumble III

Winnemucca's autobiography ⟨. . . seems⟩ to owe a good deal to preliterate autobiographical traditions. Consider how different Winnemucca's autobiography is from other early autobiographies by literate Indians. William Apes (1829), George Copway (1847), Charles Alexander Eastman (1902, 1916), and Joseph Griffis (1915) all made the journey Winnemucca made, from the tribal world to the white world. The autobiographies of Apes and Copway have at their center their conversion to Christianity. Eastman and Griffis ⟨. . .⟩ saw themselves as embodiments of Social Darwinist ideas about the progression of the races. All four of these men wrote autobiography in such a way as to describe an individual self and to account for just how that self came to be. Their autobiographies describe certain clear turning points. Had Eastman not been taken away from the Santee Sioux by his father and sent to school, he would not have become the man he became. Had Apes not found Christianity, he would have remained in a state of sin. In this way, at least, all four are typical modern autobiographers in the Western tradition.

Winnemucca has virtually nothing to say in *Life among the Piutes* about turning points. Her biographer, ⟨Gae Whitney⟩ Canfield, on the other hand, quite reasonably does include a chapter entitled "The Turning Point." The turning points are there for Western eyes to see; Winnemucca saw her life differently.

And she is again unlike modern, Western autobiographers in that she is unconcerned about self-definition. In 1870 a Sacramento reporter sought her out in a Paiute village:

> She said: I am glad to see you, although I have not now a parlor to ask you into except the one made by nature for all. I like this Indian life tolerably well; however, my only object in staying with these people is that I may do them good. I would rather be with my people, but not live as they live. I was not raised so; . . . my happiest life has been spent in Santa Clara while at school and living among the whites. (In Canfield, 1983:65)

The choices here seem to have little to do with the question of self-definition. Winnemucca enjoys living a comfortable life in the cities; when she can live in a house, she gladly does so. When she must live in a brush nobee, she is not unwilling to do so. She knows how to live in the Paiute way. She stays with her people, however, not because of a fervent love of their ways—she certainly does not stay with them because of her love of the Nevada landscape, say, or roots, or rabbit's flesh. She stays, rather, out of a sense of obligation. Winnemucca did remember some of the Paiute rituals fondly, and she may be exaggerating her altruism a bit. But this passage does seem to suggest that Winnemucca did not see the choice between the Paiute and the white way as having to do with self-definition. Eastman, Griffis, and Luther Standing Bear, on the other hand, were concerned to work out an explicit sense of who they were in relation to the two worlds they knew. Their autobiographies suggest in many ways that, in moving from prereservation Indian life to the white world, they were passing over a great divide. They speak as from a great distance of the "superstitions" of their people. Eastman and Standing Bear, especially, describe the prereservation Sioux as being simple and "childlike."

Winnemucca does not seem to see any such fundamental difference between her Indian people and the whites. Certainly she is aware of different customs; she is outraged at how dishonest the whites are, and she contrasts this with the honesty of her own people; she realizes that her people have to learn a great deal in order to become self-supporting farmers, but she nowhere suggests that there are *essential* differences. Indeed, the point of her chapter on "Domestic and Social Moralities" would seem to be that the Paiutes are *not* essentially different from whites: they are "taught to love everybody"; their women are *not* allowed to marry "until they have come to womanhood"; and, says Winnemucca, "We have a republic as well as you. The council-tent is our Congress." All of this is a part of the book's argument that the Paiutes ought to be granted land in severalty and full rights of citizenship.

Quite aside from this line of argument, Winnemucca just does not seem to see differences beyond differences in customs. Indian agent Henry Douglas wrote of Winnemucca that "She conforms readily to civilized customs, and will as readily join in an Indian dance" (Canfield, *Sarah Winnemucca of the Northern Paiutes*, 1983, 62). He would probably not have been surprised to find that she has nothing to say in *Life among the Piutes* about her conversion to Christianity; nothing, either, about a moment when she decided that, really, she preferred the white to the Paiute way. She spent time among whites; she spent time among the Paiutes. In reading her book *we* may see implicit in some of her experiences features of a cultural identity crisis, but she seems herself not to have thought about her life in this way.

—H. David Brumble III, *American Indian Autobiography* (Berkeley: University of California Press, 1988), 63–65

A. LaVonne Brown Ruoff

⟨Sarah Winnemucca⟩ was the first Indian woman writer of personal and tribal history. Like the slave narrators of the second half of the century, Winnemucca abandons the strongly Christian flavor of earlier personal narratives; unlike ⟨William⟩ Apes and ⟨George⟩ Copway, she does not pattern her narrative after spiritual confessions and missionary reminiscences. Her emphasis on personal experience as part of the ethnohistory of her tribe owes more to tribal narrative traditions than to religious ones. Further, her life history is considerably more militant than theirs.

Winnemucca's *Life among the Piutes* also differs from typical women's autobiographies. In *A Poetics of Women's Autobiography*, Sidonie Smith comments that women autobiographers deal with two stories. On the one hand, the woman autobiographer "engages in the fiction of selfhood that constitutes the discourse of man and that conveys by the way a vision of the fabricating power of male subjectivity." On the other hand, because the story of man is not exactly her story, woman's "relationship to the empowering figure of male selfhood is inevitably problematic." Matters are further complicated by the fact that she must also "engage the fictions of selfhood that constitute the idea of woman and that specify the parameters of female subjectivity, including

woman's problematic relationship to language, desire, power, and meaning."
This leads Smith to conclude that because the ideology of gender makes
woman's life history a nonstory, the ideal woman is "self-effacing rather than
self-promoting" and her "natural" story shapes itself "not around the public,
heroic life but around the fluid, circumstantial, contingent responsiveness to
others that, according to patriarchal ideology, characterizes the life of women
but not autobiography" (50).

Smith notes that when the autobiographer is a woman of color or of the
working class, she faces even more complex imbroglios of male-female figures:

> Here identities of race and class, sometimes even of nationality, inter-
> sect and confound those of gender. As a result, she is doubly or triply
> the subject of other people's representations, turned again and again
> in stories that reflect and promote certain forms of selfhood identified
> with class, race, and nationality as well as with sex. In every case,
> moreover, she remains marginalized in that she finds herself resident
> on the margins of discourse, always removed from the center of
> power within the culture she inhabits. (51)

Although marginalized within the dominant society because of her racial
heritage, Winnemucca played a central role in her tribe. ⟨. . .⟩ Far from being
marginalized, Winnemucca's role as advocate made her the mightiest word
warrior of her tribe. In "Indian Women's Personal Narrative," Kathleen Mullen
Sands concludes that Winnemucca portrays herself in opposing roles in her
autobiography: male and female, private and public: "She not only presents
herself as a warrior for Indian justice, but she also develops a portrait of a child
terrified by white power who, toward the end of her narrative, has become a
dedicated teacher of Indian pupils—a version of motherhood" (ms. 19). In
American Indian Autobiography, ⟨H. David Brumble III⟩ perceptively argues that
Life among the Piutes is a kind of coup tale in which Winnemucca records her
deeds in order to establish how she ought to be regarded, as have such Indian
men as Two Leggings and White Bull (65–66). ⟨. . .⟩

The personal characteristics Winnemucca most consistently demonstrates
are courage and stamina, particularly in her account of her role in the Bannock
War. Her exploits rival those of the western adventure tales and recall the har-
rowing experiences of the heroines of captivity and slave narratives. Between
13 and 15 June 1878, Winnemucca rode 223 miles, on horseback and by
wagon, between the Indian and army lines, in danger both from the warring
Bannocks and from whites eager to kill her for helping the Paiutes.

Winnemucca is acutely conscious that the role she played in Paiute-white
relations was unusual for a woman. In addition to the dangers encountered by
any emissary passing between enemy lines, Winnemucca and her sister Mattie,

who often accompanied her, faced the threat of rape. Warned by her cousin that whites had been lassoing Paiute women and doing "fearful" things to them, Winnemucca asserted: "If such an outrageous thing is to happen to me, it will not be done by one man or two, while there are two women with knives, for I know what an Indian can do. She can never be outraged by one man; but she may by two" (228). That Winnemucca was prepared to defend herself is illustrated by the incident in which she and her sister were forced by circumstances to share one room overnight with eight cowboys. Touched by one of them during the night, Winnemucca jumped up, punched the offender in the face, and warned: "Go away, or I will cut you to pieces, you mean man!" The startled culprit fled before she could carry out her threat (231).

Winnemucca's narrow escapes titillated the reading public's taste for both the imminence of sexuality and the triumph of virtue. The literary descendants of Pamela were expected to die rather than face dishonor, a fate they usually managed to escape. Sexual violence was a staple of both captivity and slave narratives. The women in captivity narratives trusted to their God to deliver them from the danger of rape or servitude as the captive wives of "heathen savages." If such narratives convinced whites of the innate cruelty of nonwhites, the slave narratives reminded whites of their own brutality. The degradation of slave women at the hands of masters provided the writers of slave narratives with the opportunity to demonstrate how the slave system destroyed the morality of blacks and whites. Unlike the heroines of sentimental literature or of captivity and slave narratives, Winnemucca is not a victim but rather an independent woman determined to fight off her attackers. Her strength of character, as well as a fast horse and sharp knife, enable her to achieve victories denied to her literary sisters. They also distinguish her life history from the less dramatic accounts by other women autobiographers.

—A. LaVonne Brown Ruoff, "Three Nineteenth-Century American Indian Autobiographers," in *Redefining American Literary History*, ed. A. LaVonne Brown Ruoff and Jerry W. Ward, Jr. (New York: Modern Language Association of America, 1990), 261–64

CATHERINE S. FOWLER

Sarah Winnemucca is ⟨. . .⟩ a controversial figure, and herein lies some of her historical interest. Anthropologist Robert Heizer ⟨"Notes on Some Paviotso Personalities and Material Culture," 1960, 3⟩ suggests that her "selfless motives and tremendous energies and high purpose make her a person to admire in the history of our far West." But anthropologist Omer Stewart ⟨"The Northern Paiute Bands," 1939, 129⟩ describes her as "ambitious, educated, . . . trying to attain self-aggrandizement by exalting her father." Similarly, her own people, the Northern Paiute, are of mixed opinions about her. Some recognize her

genuine achievements as the founder of an independent school and her continuing influence on those attempting to preserve an Indian voice and to
secure better conditions on local reservations. Others see her as a tool of the
military, for whom she worked at various periods in her life, and even worse,
as a traitor who caused members of her own tribe to be killed and captured in
various campaigns.

Those who read her story must judge for themselves the sum total of her
life, including the nobility of her character, the nature of her motives, and the
strength of her accomplishments. But in evaluating Sarah, one must also place
oneself as much as possible within the times and in the conditions under
which she lived and worked—not such an easy task. For example, what was
the role prescribed for a woman, let alone a Native American woman, in the
mid- to late 1800s? What could she hope to accomplish given that role and
what means were available to her? Could speaking out ever go unchallenged?

Neither written history nor oral tradition provides fully satisfactory
answers to all aspects of Sarah Winnemucca's life. She *was* an extraordinary
person. She was also a very complex person living in complex times and making complex decisions. She was of two worlds, and perhaps sadly, at home in
neither.

—Catherine S. Fowler, "Foreword" to *Life Among the Piutes: Their Wrongs and Claims* by Sarah
Winnemucca (Reno, NV: University of Nevada Press, 1994), 3–4

RUTH ROSENBERG

Throughout her book Winnemucca uses the hesitant, nonconfrontational tone
of her deferential opening sentence: "I was born somewhere near 1844, but I
am not sure of the precise time." Her third chapter opens its discussion of an
incident with the same note of caution: "This was in the year 1858, I think: I
am not sure." As a woman speaking before the time of female enfranchisement
and as a Native American lacking any rights of citizenship, she is careful not
to offend, not to recount whatever cannot be authenticated: "As I do not
remember all the particulars," she writes of one incident, "I will not attempt to
relate it."

Winnemucca also used a repertoire of stylistic devices from her oral tradition to compensate for her scanty literary background. One such feature of
storytelling performance is a shift of voice, and each of the eight chapters of
her book is narrated from a slightly altered perspective. These devices allow
Winnemucca to indicate that her narrator is growing older and that she is
increasingly assuming responsibility in situations that also grow increasingly
worse. ⟨. . .⟩

The tone of the thirty-four-year-old woman who serves as Brevet Maj. Gen. Oliver Otis Howard's guide at the outbreak of hostilities contrasts dramatically with that of the tentative, self-effacing narrator of the preceding chapters. The assured Winnemucca savors the officers' banter, thoroughly enjoys the exploits on horseback, and earns the respect of the soldiers. She reports distances ridden, troop numbers, precise times and dates; and specifies the names and ranks of members of the headquarters' staff. Her information was so accurate that when Howard wrote his autobiography in 1907 he paraphrased or quoted from her book extensively. Ferol Egan's recounting of the Pyramid Lake War also validates her accuracy, and Dorothy Nafus Morrison finds that, where discrepancies exist between the accounts of Winnemucca and the reports of newspapers, research in the archives shows the journalists in error. In his collection of chronicles by Native Americans of Nevada, Jack D. Forbes shows how reliable Winnemucca's versions are. ⟨. . .⟩

For her authoritatively detailed history and its record of the traditions of the northern Paiutes for the instruction of future generations Winnemucca earned admission to the Nevada Writers Hall of Fame in 1993. Her book serves as a significant bridge between cultures, because she had been, in the words of Patricia Stewart, "blessed with an intelligence capable of encompassing two cultures" ⟨"Sarah Winnemucca," 1971⟩.

—Ruth Rosenberg, "Sarah Winnemucca," *Dictionary of Literary Biography* 175, ed. Kenneth M. Roemer (Detroit: Gale Research, 1997), 316–17, 319–21

BIBLIOGRAPHY

Life Among the Piutes: Their Wrongs and Claims. 1883.

ZITKALA-SA

1876–1938

ZITKALA-SA was born Gertrude Simmons in 1876, the daughter of a Yankton Dakota mother, Ellen Simmons. Gertrude's father, a white man with the last name of Felker, had left the family before his daughter was born, and Ellen remarried a Sioux man named Simmons. Gertrude spent the first eight years of her life on the Yankton reservation in South Dakota. The traditions that she learned while on the reservation stayed with her, even after her years at a Quaker boarding school in Indiana, a missionary school where she learned English.

When Gertrude returned to the reservation, she was regarded with some suspicion by the Indians—she was "too white" for them to trust. She was still calling herself Gertrude, but after quarreling with her sister-in-law—who said she should give up the name Simmons because, in getting a "white" education, she had rejected her Sioux family of that name—Gertrude in response took the Indian name Zitkala-Sa. After four more years on the reservation, she left again, to finish her education at the Quaker missionary school and then to study for two years at Earlham College, also in Indiana. She later studied at the New England Conservatory of Music and had a brief but acclaimed career as a violinist, playing with the Carlisle Indian Band.

Zitkala-Sa's literary career began when she won second place in the Indiana State Oratorical Contest of 1896. The speech she delivered there, titled "Side by Side," touched on what would be the abiding themes of her other writings: the tension and difficulty of being part Native American, the inequities of the United States government's policies towards the Dakotas and other Native Americans, and the loss of the traditional way of life. Her first published work is almost an ethnographer's collection of Indian stories and folktales, published as *Old Indian Legends* (1901). Her autobiographical writings appeared in the *Atlantic Monthly* and were later collected, along with other stories and essays, in the volume *American Indian Stories* (1921).

When Zitkala-Sa married Raymond T. Bonnin in 1902, another phase of her life began—that of activist. After 14 years of living on a reservation in Utah, the couple moved to Washington, D.C., as Zitkala-Sa had been elected secretary of the Society of the American Indian, founded as a collective forum for those Native Americans who sought redress for injustices suffered through government policies. The Society dissolved in 1920, and in 1926 Zitkala-Sa founded the

National Council of American Indians, which she ran until the end of her life.

Zitkala-Sa was a controversial figure, combining self-aggrandizement (she reportedly claimed to be the granddaughter of famous Sioux leader Sitting Bull) and selflessness. Nevertheless, she is considered one of the founding voices of the Native American literary tradition. Zitkala-sa died in 1938.

C R I T I C A L   E X T R A C T S

DEXTER FISHER

To her mother and the traditional Sioux on the reservation where she had grown up, ⟨Zitkala-Sa⟩ was highly suspect because, in their minds, she had abandoned, even betrayed, the Indian way of life by getting an education in the white man's world. To those at the Carlisle Indian School where she had taught from 1898–99, on the other hand, she was an anathema because she insisted on remaining "Indian," writing embarrassing articles such as "Why I am A Pagan" that flew in the face of the assimilationist thrust of their education. A particularly bitter review of one of her stories appears in the 12 April, 1901 edition of *The Red Man and Helper*, Carlisle's newspaper, with this prefatory note:

> All that Zitkalasa has in the way of literary ability and culture she owes to the good people, who, from time to time, have taken her into their homes and hearts and given her aid. Yet not a word of gratitude or allusion to such kindness on the part of her friends has ever escaped her in any line of anything she has written for the public. By this course she injures herself and harms the educational work in progress for the race from which she sprang. In a list of educated Indians whom we have in mind, some of whom have reached higher altitudes in literary and professional lines than Zitkalasa, we know of no other case of such pronounced morbidness.

The reviewer goes on to pronounce the story in question, "The Soft-hearted Sioux," morally bad. And why so? Because it challenges the very core of educational policy at Carlisle. A fictional account of the inadequacy of off-reservation schools to prepare Indians to live within their own cultures, the story is told in the first person by a young Sioux who describes the conflict he experiences in being unable to fulfill his father's desire that he become a warrior and huntsman because he has spent nine years at a missionary school and "hunted for the soft heart of Christ, and prayed for the huntsman who chased the buffalo on the plains."

Despite its sentimentality, the story raises the fundamental question of survival that was to confront all Indians educated off the reservation. What price assimilation?

For Zitkala Sa, the conflict between tradition and acculturation was to plague her throughout her life. Born as Gertrude Simmons on the Yankton Reservation in South Dakota in 1876, she spent her first eight years of life on the reservation with her mother in a seemingly idyllic state of harmony, as she describes in "Impressions of an Indian Childhood," published in *The Atlantic Monthly* in 1900:

> I was a wild little girl of seven. Loosely clad in a slip of brown buckskin, and light footed with a pair of soft moccasins on my feet, I was as free as the wind that blew my hair, and no less spirited than a bounding deer. These were my mother's pride—my wild freedom and over flowing spirit.

Educated in the traditions of the Sioux, she listened to the legends at night and learned to imitate her mother's bead work during the day. Though her mother had been married to three different white men and had lived at times off the reservation, she never learned to speak English and retained always the Sioux way of life. When Gertrude's father, a man named Felker, deserted the family before his daughter's birth, the mother decided to return to the Yankton agency to live. She also determined to give Gertrude the name of her second husband, Simmons. Gertrude christened herself Zitkala Sa, Red Bird, when she had a falling out with her sister-in-law. 〈. . .〉 In creating her own name and essentially her own oral history, Zitkala Sa is asserting at one and the same time her independence and her cultural ties. As Zitkala Sa, she will try to recreate the spirit of her tribe in her collection of legends, though she is never able to return to Yankton permanently.

—Dexter Fisher, "Zitkala Sa: The Evolution of a Writer," *American Indian Quarterly* 5, no. 3 (August 1979): 230–32

AGNES M. PICOTTE

The legends are told in an easy, engaging style with a certain dramatic power. Zitkala-Sa heard them as a child, and she carefully selected each story to appeal to her audiences of all ages, who were the children of the world. She was a most imaginative author, deeply concerned with beauty. She felt keenly throughout her formal education that she represented her race in everything she wrote. The 165 pages of *Old Indian Legends* contain fourteen stories filled with figures like Iktomi or Unktomi, the snare weaver, the cunning trickster whose tricks sometimes backfired. Iktomi-spider is an unconventional character who breaks all the rules of conduct and tradition. Many times he is purely foolish.

Eya also enters into the stories. He is the eater, the glutton who has magical powers. Able to deceive people in order to devour them, he is portrayed as a giant with a huge stomach and spindly legs. However, he is stupid and easily fooled. Another figure, Anuk-ite, or Old Double Face, is a giant with large, funnel-like ears. He is a cruel and evil person who delights in making children suffer. Lingering on the outskirts of camps waiting to snatch children away who might be out for any reason, he throws these children in his ears and takes them away to some secluded place to torture them. The Blood Clot boy is also a magical figure. He is a hero in the time of great need. The animal stories personify certain animals that are evil and others that are good.

Old Indian Legends draws on the oral tradition of storytelling in the Sioux Nation. Each narrator used his or her own style and personality to embellish each story according to his or her talents. The *ohunkankans* were told in the evening as everyone in the family went to bed, during the time between lying down and sleep. Any person in the family could be the storyteller, but mostly it was a grandparent or some other experienced person. Many times one distinguished for good *ohunkankans* was sought after, made a relative if not already one, and invited to be a guest for a month or any length of time so that he or she could tell *ohunkankans* to that particular family. Often a story could be continued for a few evenings or weeks on end. Thus the stories, customs, and legends were kept alive. Zitkala-Sa would help keep them alive by recording them.

—Agnes M. Picotte, "Foreword" to *Old Indian Legends* by Zitkala-Sa (Lincoln: University of Nebraska Press, 1985), xiii–xv

DOROTHEA M. SUSAG

From the very beginning of "Impressions of an Indian Childhood," Zitkala-Sa gives voice to a theme that Euro-American society had previously ignored or suppressed: the strength and essential value of women in the traditional Lakota world. Behind the printed images of women roams the wily Iktomi, disguised as a white cultural imperialist, who would have Indian women believe they are the "quiet and passive drudges" of society, "beasts of burden," and inferior to Indian men, as long as they remain "uncivilized" ⟨Katherine Weist, "Beasts of Burden and Menial Slaves," 1983, 29⟩. However, despite Gertrude Simmons

Bonnin's life-long conflict with her home community, and especially with her mother, these essays work to outsmart Iktomi, by defending and honoring her mother, and by celebrating the strength of Indian women, even as they live midst the clash of two cultures.

As we read these essays against ⟨Edward Said's concept of⟩ the memory of a traditional landscape, the voices of Lakota women resound to defy the Trickster with their own definitions of Indian women. A Santee woman once told Ella Deloria the characteristics of a "good [Lakota] woman":

> . . . devoted to her children, industrious and skilled in womanly arts, genuinely hospitable and generous, and a strict follower of kinship etiquette. She should think much but say little, and she should stay at home and occupy herself with her own business. ⟨Raymond DeMallie, "Male and Female in Traditional Lakota Culture," 1983, 260⟩

Beatrice Medicine, a Lakota anthropologist and niece of Ella Deloria, considers the traditional roles of Indian women not as subservient to men but complementary, equally powerful, and viable today; she provides a more comprehensive definition of Lakota feminine power:

> "We are the carriers of culture." This belief may provide Indian women a mandate to transmit cultural viability, engendering a sense of identity with a unique and satisfying cultural group. It is this that gives Lakota women the strength to operate in both the native and the non-native life spheres. ⟨"Indian Women and the Renaissance of Traditional Medicine," 1987, 171⟩

Against the memory of a Dakota landscape, the word and image of the Euro-American's patriarchal and paternalistic belief system explode into Dakota metaphor. From the very beginning through her word and presence, *Tate I Yohin Win* sends her power and the power of her feminine Dakotah ancestors to her daughter, Zitkala-Sa.

> . . . she patted my head and said, "Now let me see how fast you can run today." Whereupon, I tore away at my highest possible speed, with my long black hair blowing in the breeze. (*Stories* 8)

It is the power manifested in her name and in the feminine Wind, *Tate*, the extraordinary and no less powerful Lakota force that moves in connection with the masculine Sky, *Skan*. It moves in their "dwelling," when "cool morning breezes" sweep from the prairie. With her hair "blowing in the breeze," the child physically knows this power that whispers to clouds, roars around mountain tops, and drives her spirit as she runs "free as the wind . . . no less spirited than a bounding deer." With pride, her mother watches her daughter's "wild freedom and overflowing spirits." In Zitkala-Sa's recollection and recording of this image, she acknowledges her mother's personification of this most powerful force, and she affirms the continuity between the Wind, her mother, and herself.

> —Dorothea M. Susag, "Zitkala-Sa (Gertrude Simmons Bonnin): A Power(full) Literary Voice," *Studies in American Indian Literatures* 5, no. 4 (Winter 1993): 10–11

PATRICIA OKKER

The complexities of canonization are ⟨. . .⟩ emphasized when one considers that the same qualities that keep "The Soft-Hearted Sioux" outside the canons of American realism and naturalism suggest its connections with another canon—namely that of American women's writings. Judith Fetterley and Marjorie Pryse have recently placed Zitkala-Sa ⟨. . .⟩ in the tradition of American women regionalists, whom they distinguish from local color writers: "[I]n practice the regionalists did differentiate themselves from the 'local colorists,' primarily in their desire not to hold up regional characters to potential ridicule by eastern urban readers but to present regional experience from within, so as to engage the reader's sympathy and identification." Because regionalists work from within the culture they describe, they often demand the kind of emotional connection between reader and subject found in Zitkala-Sa's "The Soft-Hearted Sioux." As Fetterley and Pryse explain, "regionalist texts allow the reader to view the regional speaker as subject and not as object and to include empathic feeling as an aspect of critical response" ⟨*American Women Regionalists, 1850–1910: A Norton Anthology*, 1992, xii, xvii⟩.

Fetterley and Pryse's association of local color with writing by white men but regionalism with that by women and some minority writers suggests that race—in addition to gender—influences a writer's decision to write from within a culture. Such is certainly the case with Zitkala-Sa's "The Soft-Hearted Sioux." Told from the perspective of the dying Sioux rather than a detached observer, this is a story of considerable melodrama. Zitkala-Sa's similarities with her narrator—they are both caught between two cultures—heighten the writer's and reader's empathy with the narrator. Significantly, the kind of detached, outside observation notable in realistic fiction parallels the perspective of the early twentieth-century ethnographers. Given the racial biases of early twentieth-century ethnography, Zitkala-Sa may well have intentionally chosen a more personal perspective for her fiction.

It is precisely this perspective of writing from within Sioux culture that establishes Zitkala-Sa's place within the tradition of Native American literatures. Although Zitkala-Sa is hardly considered a major figure within that tradition, as it is presently being defined, her story "A Warrior's Daughter" has been included in Paula Gunn Allen's recent collection, *Spider Woman's Granddaughters*. This story differs significantly from "The Soft-Hearted Sioux," yet again, the same features that exclude it from canonical realism place it well within Native American literatures. Its grand and dramatic portrayal of a young girl killing one of her lover's enemies and then rescuing the captured lover makes it an unlikely candidate for either realism or naturalism. At the same time, however, these same characteristics connect the story, as Allen suggests, with traditional tales of women warriors.

—Patricia Okker, "Native American Literatures and the Canon," in *American Realism and the Canon*, ed. Tom Quirk and Gary Scharnhorst (Newark, DE: University of Delaware Press, 1994), 94–95

ELIZABETH AMMONS

When we say American realism, two immediate questions are: Whose reality? And: Whose America? ⟨. . .⟩

⟨Paula Gunn⟩ Allen advocates the obvious ⟨strategy for expanding the canon of American realism⟩—starting over.

> Perhaps the best course is to begin anew, to examine the literary output of American writers of whatever stripe and derive critical principles based on what is actually being rendered by the true experts, the writers themselves. While we're at it, we might take a look at the real America that most of us inhabit—the one seldom approached by denizens of the hallowed (or is it hollow?) groves of academe—so that we can discover what is being referenced beyond abstractions familiar to establishment types but foreign to those who live in real time. I am suggesting a critical system that is founded on the principle of inclusion rather than on that of exclusion, on actual human society and relationships rather than on textual relations alone, a system that is soundly based on aesthetics that pertain to the literatures we wish to examine. ⟨"Border Studies," 1992, 309⟩

Allen's advice, for me, means building a definition of American realism not simply on William Dean Howells's famous prescriptions for realists, grounded as they are in white, middle-class ideas about what is ordinary, common, and representative of the lives of actual men and women in the United States, but also on Charles Chesnutt's articulations of what it means as an African American writer to try to render "reality"; Zitkala-Sa's definition of Sioux reality in *Old Indian Legends*, as well as her representation of mixed cultural realities in her autobiographical writing; and Sui Sin Far's fictional and autobiographical definitions of the "real" from her particular Chinese American point of view. In other words, to follow Allen's advice and start over with a truly heterogeneous set of writers, works, and life conditions is to arrive at a new conceptualization of American realism as a multiple rather than a unitary phenomenon, American realism as American realisms. ⟨. . .⟩

Old Indian Legends ⟨. . . .⟩ presents a single cultural reality, which is Sioux. Although the book exists in print and is written in English, it claims a place in Anglo-derived United States literature for a Native American, which is to say, a nonwestern, work of art. And Zitkala-Sa makes that claim in full awareness of her narratives' prior and prime identity on the North American continent. As she states in her preface: "I have tried to transplant the native spirit of these tales—root and all—into the English language, since America in the last few centuries has acquired a second tongue" ⟨1985, xi⟩.

Everything about *Old Indian Legends* challenges standard academic notions about American realism. Its announced, intended audience of children says that it cannot be "serious" literature (even though *Huckleberry Finn*, of course, is); and this announcement is reinforced by Zitkala-Sa's simplicity of language and presentation, her main characters' embodiment as animals, and the protagonist's identity as trickster—all of which distance and confuse the reader taught to expect and admire Henry James. Most disorienting, perhaps, is the complete, uncommented-upon absence of white people in *Old Indian Legends*— and with them the complete absence of any Judeo-Christian frame of reference. How do western-trained readers read this book? As Arnold Krupat, addressing the issue of academic critical methodology and Native American texts, points out, "Native American cultural production is based upon a profound wisdom that is most certainly different from a Western, rationalistic, scientistic, secular perspective" ⟨*The Voice in the Margin*, 1989, 14⟩. This leads me (despite Krupat's argument to the contrary) to try different ways of proceeding, ways that bring into the classroom oral and communal experiences of literature in addition to individual, analytic thinking.

Certainly, it is important to contextualize *Old Indian Legends* by providing conventional academic lectures and discussions that focus on Sioux culture and history, including, in particular, information about the Massacre at Wounded Knee, which occurred just eleven years before Zitkala-Sa's book and must have exerted a major influence on her decision to issue a collection of traditional tales. Also, because the subject has been so neglected, in most United States classrooms some formal lecturing is necessary to introduce students to the activity of thinking seriously about Native American literary traditions, values, and aesthetic principles. Still, a text such as *Old Indian Legends* demands more than just intellectualizing. Without falling into sentimental, bogus attempts to "be" Indian, the approach to this text needs, in some way, to stretch students' awareness. In representing Sioux reality independent of European presence, *Old Indian Legends* asserts a cultural integrity and strength— an indestructableness—which stands at the very core of this book's realism. Iktomi the trickster constantly changes shapes, plans, plots, roles, locations, faces, bodies, jokes, schemes, fates, and futures. But all of this contradictori- ness coheres in one created principle within one complex universe that embraces—weblike—all worlds, visible and invisible. Artistic principles of repetition, laughter, silence, orality, and cyclicness reinforce Zitkala-Sa's real- ism of multivocal creational wholeness and continuity, a realism both reflected in and productive of this book.

    —Elizabeth Ammons, "Expanding the Canon of American Realism," in *The Cambridge Companion to American Realism and Naturalism: Howells to London*, ed. Donald Pizer (New York: Cambridge University Press, 1995), 95, 102–3, 110–11

B I B L I O G R A P H Y

Old Indian Legends, Retold by Zitkala-Sa. 1901.

American Indian Stories. 1921.

Oklahoma's Poor Rich Indians: An Orgy of Graft and Exploitation of the Five Civilized Tribes—Legalized Robbery. 1924.